C O N T E N T S

REDISCOVERING YOU

A JOURNEY THROUGH SELF-LOVE, PURPOSE AND INNER STRENGTH

QUAN THOMAS

Published by:
JM Publishing LLC
www.jmpublishingllc.com

Cover Design by JM Publishing LLC
Interior Design by JM Publishing LLC

Printed in the United States of America.

ISBN: 979-8-9925359-2-1
First Edition: 2024

For more information, please contact:
quan@quanthomas.com

DEDICATION

This book is dedicated to every soul who dares to pause, reflect, and reclaim the pieces of themselves they've lost along the way — this book is for YOU.

May these words be a mirror, a guide, and a reminder that your true self has always been within reach.

You are not alone on this journey.

You are worthy of rediscovery.

You are worthy of YOU.

INTRODUCTION

Welcome to *Rediscovering You: A Journey through Self-Love, Purpose, and Inner Strength*. This book is a guide, a companion, and a gentle reminder that the path to transformation begins within. Whether you're feeling stuck, struggling with adversity, or simply yearning for more, this journey will help you uncover the potential lying dormant inside you and equip you with the tools to live with purpose, joy, and authenticity.

Life has a way of pulling us in many directions, leaving us worn out and often disconnected from the very core of who we are. I've been here many times before. In striving to meet everyone else's expectations, we sometimes lose sight of our own dreams and values. We silence our needs and wants, convincing ourselves that they aren't as important as our responsibilities or the opinions of others. But deep down, we know there's a part of us yearning to break free from these limits and reconnect with what truly matters. Often, what we don't understand is how we get there.

This journey isn't about quick fixes or shortcuts. Instead, it's about meaningful growth and transformation.

It's about courageously facing the stories we've believed about ourselves, understanding the pain we carry, and using that awareness to create a life that aligns with our values, passions, and purpose. I know it may seem difficult, but you deserve this. In these pages, you'll be guided through experiences and insights designed to help you understand your unique path, build resilience, and reclaim your self-worth.

Each chapter in this book will take you deeper into the journey of rediscovery, exploring topics like recognizing the signs of self-neglect, embracing vulnerability, building resilience, and shaping a vision for a life filled with purpose and fulfillment. Along the way, you'll find journal prompts to encourage reflection, challenging you to look inward and engage with your own story. These prompts aren't just exercises; they are invitations to be honest with yourself and confront the shadows and the strengths within.

Rediscovering You is here to remind you that your past, with all its challenges and setbacks, does not define you. Instead, **YOU** hold the power to reshape your life by the choices you make, the beliefs **YOU** embrace, and the self-compassion **YOU** practice. This book will show you how to turn life's trials into tools for growth, resilience, and self-love. It's a call to see yourself, not as the sum of your circumstances but as capable of change, hope, and transformation.

The road ahead may not always be easy, but remember, you're not alone. Let's start the journey back to YOU step by step, page by page, with courage, compassion, and a renewed commitment to rediscovering your true self. You were never lost—just waiting to be reminded of the divine light within you. This journey isn't just about rediscovery, it's about *reconnection*—to God, to purpose, and to whom you were always created to be. If you're reading this, your healing has already begun.

"I honor the truth I've been avoiding,
and I'm ready to face myself with love."

FACING THE MIRROR: HOW DID YOU GET HERE?

"To understand where you're going, you
must first see where you stand. Reflection
is the first step toward transformation."
—Quan Thomas

L ife doesn't always go as planned. Most of us, myself
included, set out with ambitions and dreams, motivated
by an idea of who we want to become, the life we want,
and what we want to achieve. Yet, somewhere along the
way, it's become easy to lose ourselves in the expectations of
others. Eventually, many of us reach a point where we feel
as if we're simply surviving, not thriving, moving through
each day on autopilot, missing the spark that once lit our
life's journey. *I call it burnout.*

For some, the feeling sneaks in quietly and takes years to recognize because it is disguised in familiar daily routines. For others, it's a loud wake-up call, a moment of reckoning like a sudden health scare, family issues, betrayal, or something dramatic where everything comes crashing down. However it arrives, this realization brings one pressing question: **How did I get here?**

I can tell you, as I'm a living witness to this. We told ourselves we're too busy or that "one day" we'll get back to taking care of ourselves and reconnecting with our dreams. But that day rarely comes without intention. Instead, we find ourselves perpetually running on empty, overextended, and exhausted, trying to please everyone and meet every expectation except our own. We become strangers to ourselves, defined more by roles and responsibilities than by our dreams, values, or desires. That's how we got here.

I was doing it all—holding everyone together, meeting deadlines, running errands, cooking, showing up. I was performing life like a professional. From the outside, I looked strong. But inside? I was unraveling.

I remember standing in the kitchen one afternoon, hands full, phone ringing, dinner half-prepped—and suddenly I just stopped. My hands were shaking. My chest felt tight. I couldn't breathe. There were no tears yet, just silence. No one around. No one checking in.

That was the moment it hit me: I wasn't just tired. I was empty. I had poured out so much of myself into everyone and everything else that I forgot to leave anything for me. And the worst part? I didn't even know how long it had been since I felt like *myself*

I stopped everything, turned everything off and looked at myself in the mirror. Exhausted, eyes hollow, spirit heavy. I didn't recognize the woman staring back at me. She looked like she had it all together on the outside, but on the inside? She was disappearing.

The mirror didn't lie. It reflected everything I had been hiding. I had poured myself into everyone and everything else—work, obligations, appearances—until there was barely anything left for me. I was the strong one. The dependable one. The one who didn't break. But the truth? I was breaking. Quietly. Secretly.

That moment didn't feel like strength. It felt like surrender. But it was also the beginning. I whispered, "God… where did I go?" And somehow, just asking the question cracked something open in me.

For me, initially, I didn't understand. I just knew I didn't like the mirror image gazing back at me. Every day wasn't a day I looked forward to, and pulling the covers over my eyes became the norm. This nagging sense of anxiety pressured me to keep up and stay ahead. I'd felt these feelings before, and they were increasing persistently as if I was in a chokehold. This time I heard my inner voice: "YOU'RE DOING TOO MUCH," but it was all I knew. Doing too much. All the years of neglecting myself resulted in everything shutting down. After all the outpouring I'd done, now I wondered, *How in the world would someone pour back into me?*

Maybe you are in or have experienced a low point, a period in life where you couldn't imagine things getting any more complicated, any heavier. You told yourself, "This must be the bottom," only to find that the struggles continued—as if life itself was testing how much you could handle. When faced with these moments, it's easy to feel powerless and trapped in circumstances beyond our control. But the truth is, this moment of awareness— this recognition that things aren't as they should be—is a powerful turning point. It's the first step on the path to rediscovery. If you're reading this and you've had your own mirror moment—whether literal or emotional—please hear me: you're not weak, and you're not too far gone. The fact that you're aware means you've already started the journey back to yourself. You may feel lost right now, but God never lost sight of you. And neither have I.

If this sounds familiar, know that you're not alone. Countless others have reached this same breaking point, realizing that they've been giving and giving until there's nothing left. This moment, though painful, is also an invitation. It's a call to stop, breathe, and begin the journey back to yourself.

Today, no matter where you are in life, I want you to start honoring your journey and examining the steps that brought you to this moment. It's the beginning of an exploration into the self, an opportunity to ask hard questions, confront old patterns, and make space for a new beginning.

Mirror Truth: "I am no longer available for anything that makes me disappear."

The Weight of Expectations

As children, we're often encouraged to dream big, to imagine all the wonderful things we'll do and the person we'll become. But as we grow older, the freedom of childhood dreams begins to compete with societal expectations, familial responsibilities, and cultural narratives. We're told what success looks like, how we should behave, and what roles we're expected to play. These expectations can be subtle, yet they become deeply ingrained, shaping our decisions and influencing how we see ourselves. Over time, these external demands can overshadow our inner voice, guiding us down paths that might feel safe or predictable but leave us hollow.

For many, this disconnection starts small. Perhaps you took a job you didn't want because it offered stability, or maybe you stayed in a relationship because you felt it was the "right" thing to do. Whatever it was, it helped you decide to hang on while it drained the energy from you. To the point where you couldn't recognize yourself. Bit by bit, the dreams you once held close began to fade, replaced by a sense of duty or obligation. It's easy to fall into routines that feel comforting but ultimately keep us stagnant. We tell ourselves that one day we'll make time for our passions or pursue our dreams. But for now, we'll simply go through the motions. This includes the motions of not taking care of ourselves.

This slow, drifting away from our true selves often happens so gradually that we hardly notice it. Yet, one day we look in the mirror and realize the person staring back is not who we thought we would become. We feel the weight of unfulfilled dreams, the fatigue of overextension, and the emptiness that comes from ignoring our true desires. The first step in rediscovering yourself is recognizing the expectations that have guided you and questioning whether they truly align with who you want to be.

The Illusion of Perfection

A significant barrier to self-discovery is the illusion of perfection. Society tends to celebrate success stories, polished images, and achievements that fit a certain mold. We then secretly feel as though we have to live up to that. This creates the pressure to conform, to present ourselves as having it all together even when we don't. We strive for perfection in our careers, relationships, and even in personal growth. But this perfection is often a facade, masking the struggles, setbacks, and insecurities that are a natural part of the human experience.

Embracing imperfection is a radical act of self-love. It means acknowledging that growth is messy, mistakes are inevitable, and progress is not always linear. The pressure to appear perfect can be paralyzing, causing us to delay our dreams and avoid taking risks out of fear of failure. But perfection is an illusion, an unattainable standard that ultimately leaves us feeling inadequate and drained.

Rediscovering yourself requires letting go of the need to be flawless. It means permitting yourself to be human, make mistakes, and learn from them. This vulnerability is not a weakness but a strength, a willingness to show up authentically even when uncomfortable. By embracing imperfection, you create space for growth and invite a more genuine connection with yourself and others.

Identifying the Patterns That Keep You Stuck

Another critical aspect of self-discovery is examining the patterns that have shaped your life. We all have habits, routines, and thought processes that we often fall into without realizing it. Some of these patterns serve us well, providing stability and consistency. However, others may keep us stuck, limiting our potential and holding us back from true fulfillment.

Think about the routines you follow each day. Do they bring you closer to your goals, or are they simply a way to get by? Think about the beliefs you hold about yourself. Are they empowering, or do they reinforce self-doubt? These patterns are often deeply ingrained, rooted in past experiences, and shaped by the environments we grew up in. They can be challenging to break, but the first step is awareness.

Start by asking yourself some difficult questions:

- What habits no longer serve me?
- What beliefs are holding me back?
- What relationships drain my energy instead of nourishing it?

These questions may be uncomfortable, but they're essential for breaking free from patterns that keep you in a cycle of unfulfillment. Recognizing these patterns is a form of liberation, a chance to reclaim your life and make choices that align with your true self.

The Consequences of Self-Neglect

As humans, some of us have a natural tendency to ignore ourselves. We put "US" on the back burner. When we ignore our needs, we send a message to ourselves that we are not worth prioritizing. Self-neglect often goes unnoticed at first, as we pour our energy into caring for others, meeting responsibilities, or chasing external markers of success. But over time, this neglect takes a toll, manifesting as burnout, resentment, or a sense of emptiness. We may find ourselves feeling physically exhausted, emotionally drained, or mentally uninspired.

Self-neglect doesn't just impact our well-being; it also diminishes our sense of identity. When we constantly put others' needs above our own, we lose touch with our desires, passions, and individuality. The journey to rediscovery involves recognizing where you've been sacrificing yourself and consciously deciding to prioritize self-care. This isn't about being selfish; it's about respecting your own needs and acknowledging that you cannot pour from an empty cup.

Reflect on the areas in your life where you've been neglecting yourself. Are there passions you've put on hold? Relationships you've outgrown? Dreams you've dismissed as impractical? Reclaiming these aspects of yourself is a powerful act of self-love, a declaration that your happiness and well-being are worth fighting for.

Expanding the View on Self-Neglect

We don't realize that self-neglect often extends beyond career pressures or relationship dynamics. It shows up in various areas of life that might be easily overlooked. By recognizing these broader forms of neglect early, we become more attuned to areas that might need nurturing, creating a foundation for a more balanced, fulfilled life.

1. ***Creative and Intellectual Neglect***: Many people lose touch with their creative interests, passions, or curiosity, viewing these pursuits as "non-essential." Over time, this leads to stagnation and can diminish feelings of excitement or purpose. For example, an individual who once loved playing music may ignore this passion due to work demands, losing a vital form of self-expression.

2. ***Environmental Neglect***: The spaces we inhabit reflect our mental and emotional states. Ignoring our living environment by letting clutter pile up or avoiding organizing can create stress and overwhelm us. An untidy space might feel like a minor issue, but it often signals larger patterns of self-neglect and may impact our overall well-being.

3. ***Physical and Sensory Neglect***: Neglecting the need for physical comfort and sensory enjoyment is common. Simple acts, such as enjoying time in nature, taking a warm bath, or wearing clothes that feel good, help ground us and can contribute to a positive self-image. Ignoring these needs may lead to burnout, increased stress, and a weakened connection to one's body and senses.

Recognizing these diverse forms of self-neglect reminds us that self-care extends beyond basic needs and responsibilities; it's about honoring every aspect of ourselves. Practicing self-discovery makes us aware of the areas in our lives where small, intentional changes can rekindle joy, growth, and fulfillment.

The Role of Self-Compassion in Rediscovery

One of the most critical lessons in the journey to rediscovery is learning to be kind to yourself. We are often our own harshest critics, holding ourselves to impossible standards and punishing ourselves for mistakes. For me, I found myself beating myself up all the time. Arguing, fighting, and saying many mean things to myself. This self-criticism created a cycle of shame and self-doubt, which made it difficult for me to move forward. During these times, we must find compassion within ourselves. Self-compassion is a transformative practice that allows us to acknowledge our imperfections without judgment. We should treat ourselves with the same kindness that we would offer a friend or loved one.

Self-compassion is not about ignoring our faults or making excuses but recognizing our humanity. It means acknowledging that everyone struggles, everyone makes mistakes, and growth is a continuous process. This includes you! Practicing self-compassion can be challenging, especially if you're used to being hard on yourself. But by cultivating this kindness, you create a foundation for genuine change.

While it's often said that "if you knew better you would do better" in moments of self-doubt, remind yourself that you are doing the best you can with the knowledge and resources you have. Offer yourself the grace to grow, stumble, and learn along the way. The same grace you would show a child trying to figure things out. This compassion is not only a gift to yourself but a necessary step toward reconnecting with your authentic self.

Taking Ownership of Your Story

The journey to rediscovery is ultimately about reclaiming ownership of your life. It's about taking responsibility for your choices, recognizing the power you have to shape your future, and honoring the unique path that brought you here. This doesn't mean blaming yourself for past mistakes or dwelling on regrets; instead, it's acknowledging the lessons learned and using them as stepping stones to move forward.

Owning your story means embracing all parts of yourself: the successes, failures, dreams fulfilled, and dreams deferred. It means recognizing that every experience has contributed to the person you are today, no matter how painful or challenging. By taking ownership, you empower yourself to make changes, rewrite old narratives, and create a life that aligns with your values and passions.

Journal Reflection: How Did I Get Here?

As we close this first chapter, I invite you to reflect on the journey that brought you here. Take out your journal and answer the following questions with honesty and compassion:

1. What areas of my life feel out of alignment with my true self?
2. Are there expectations I've been carrying that no longer serve me?
3. What patterns or habits keep me feeling stuck?
4. How have I been neglecting my needs, and what impact has that had on my well-being?
5. In what ways can I start showing more compassion for myself?

These questions are a starting point, a way to peel back the layers beneath your roles and responsibilities and reconnect with the person you are. As you explore these reflections, remember that this journey is not about perfection but progress. No matter how small, each insight brings you one step closer to rediscovering the person you were always meant to be.

In the following chapters we'll continue to build on these reflections, diving deeper into self-discovery, healing, and growth. But for now, give yourself permission to be here—to honor the journey you've taken and open yourself to the possibilities that lie ahead. This is the beginning of a new chapter, a new commitment to yourself. Embrace it, and let the journey unfold.

"I choose to make myself a priority—
without guilt, without apology."

CHAPTER 2

AWAKENING TO SELF-CARE

"You cannot pour from an empty
cup. Recognize when you need
care, for nurturing yourself is the
foundation of all growth."
—Quan Thomas

As we peel back the layers of our lives, one of the hardest truths to confront is the subtle, often invisible signs of self-neglect. These signs aren't always dramatic; they rarely appear as an abrupt breakdown or a life-altering crisis. Instead, self-neglect builds slowly over time, woven into the fabric of our daily routines, relationships, and responsibilities. While it took years for me to understand what was happening, the breakdown seemed abrupt, but truly, it had been a long time coming. That's what happens to many of us. We might not even notice it occurring until we feel an emptiness that can't be explained, a fatigue that rest can't fix, or a disconnection from the things that once brought us joy. We find that there's no outlet anymore, and we become trapped or stop doing it altogether. I used to believe self-care was optional. Something I'd get around to when everything else was done. But everything else was *never* done.

One night, I was folding laundry late, with emails unread, texts piling up, and my body aching. I walked into the bathroom, caught my reflection—and instead of seeing exhaustion, I saw resentment. Not toward anyone else, but toward myself. For allowing things to get this far. That night, I sat on the floor and cried. Not because of the laundry, or the work—but because I realized I hadn't asked myself, 'What do *you* need?' in a long, long time. That night, I chose to stop. I lit a candle. I took a long bath. I prayed. It wasn't extravagant—but it was the first thing I had done for me in weeks. And that one small decision reminded me:

Healing doesn't begin with big changes—it begins with permission

The effects of self-neglect show up in every area of life. When we constantly push through exhaustion and ignore our need for rest, reflection, or emotional care, it begins to affect how we show up at work, in our relationships, and with ourselves. Mental fatigue, low motivation, and emotional burnout are often signs that we've been putting everything and everyone else first for too long.

Self-neglect is an insidious force. It can disguise itself as diligence, responsibility, or even compassion. We convince ourselves that we're just being productive, making sacrifices for the good of others, or that we're too busy to pause and care for ourselves. But in truth, this neglect slowly erodes our sense of self-worth, joy, and ultimately, our capacity to thrive.

The Many Faces of Self-Neglect

Self-neglect doesn't always look the way we expect. We often think of it as a complete disregard for self-care or physical needs, but it can manifest in more subtle, nuanced ways. Here are some common forms of self-neglect that often go unrecognized:

1. *Physical Neglect:* This is the most visible form of self-neglect, yet it often goes unaddressed. It might appear as poor eating habits, lack of exercise, or neglecting regular health checkups. We justify these choices with excuses like being "too busy" or "too tired," but over time, these habits take a toll on our bodies and subsequently, our energy and mood. A healthy body supports a healthy mind, yet when we neglect our physical health, we

slowly drain ourselves, reducing our resilience and capacity to handle daily stresses.

Example: Think about the last time you skipped a workout or opted for fast food because you didn't have time to cook. At that moment, it may have felt like the easier choice. However, these small decisions can become a habit over time, and we may wake up one day realizing that we haven't prioritized our health in years.

2. ***Emotional Neglect***: This form of neglect involves ignoring or suppressing our feelings. We may bottle up emotions, avoid difficult conversations, or refuse to acknowledge our needs and desires. Emotional neglect creates a buildup of unprocessed feelings that can lead to anxiety, stress, and even depression. When we don't give our emotions the space they need, they can feel overwhelming or unmanageable.

Example: Consider the last time you felt hurt, angry, or disappointed but didn't address those feelings. Maybe you told yourself you were overreacting or didn't want to burden others. But ignoring these emotions doesn't make them go away; it simply pushes them below the surface, where they can quietly drain your energy.

3. *Mental Neglect*: When we stop challenging ourselves mentally, we open the door to emotions that leave us stagnant and uninspired. This can look like avoiding activities that once excited us, neglecting personal growth, or spending excessive time on mindless tasks to escape from deeper issues. Mental neglect can disconnect us from our sense of purpose and curiosity.

   Example: Think about a hobby or interest you used to enjoy but haven't made time for recently. Whether reading, writing, solving puzzles, or learning something new, these activities fuel our minds and keep us engaged with the world around us. Without them, life can feel monotonous and uninspired.

4. *Social Neglect*: This is often overlooked, especially for those who see themselves as independent or self-reliant. Social neglect might mean isolating ourselves, avoiding meaningful connections, or failing to nurture relationships that once mattered to us. Over time, social neglect can lead to loneliness and isolation, diminishing our sense of belonging and support.

   Example: Reflect on the last time you reached out to a friend, shared a meaningful conversation, or participated in a community activity. Social interactions are vital for emotional well-being, and prolonged isolation can increase feelings of loneliness, which may affect our mental and physical health.

5. ***Spiritual Neglect***: Spiritual neglect is less about "religion" and more about a disconnection from meaning or purpose. It could mean ignoring practices that give us a sense of peace, purpose, or inner connection, such as meditation, prayer, spending time in nature, or reflecting on our values. When we neglect our spiritual well-being, we may feel adrift, as if our lives lack depth and direction.

    Example: Consider your own spiritual practices, whatever they may be. It could be something as simple as a moment of gratitude, journaling, or connecting with nature. Without these practices, life can feel shallow or disconnected from a larger purpose.

These five forms of neglect are interconnected, and when one area suffers, it often impacts the others. For example, emotional neglect can lead to physical neglect as we turn to unhealthy coping mechanisms. Social neglect can exacerbate feelings of isolation, impacting our mental and emotional health. Recognizing these patterns is the first step in addressing self-neglect and restoring balance in our lives.

You may have recognized yourself in more than one of these. That doesn't make you weak—it makes you *aware*. And awareness is power. If you're someone who's always giving, always managing, always smiling even when your soul is heavy—please know this: you are not selfish for needing care. You are not dramatic for needing rest. And you are not broken for needing time to reconnect with you.

The Warning Signs of Self-Neglect

Self-neglect often reveals itself through a series of subtle but persistent warning signs. These signs may vary from person to person, but here are some common indicators to watch for:

1. ***Exhaustion that Rest Doesn't Fix***: Feeling constantly tired, even after sleep, is a common sign of burnout and self-neglect. It's a signal that your body and mind are running on empty, unable to recharge because you're consistently ignoring your needs. This exhaustion can be emotional as well as physical, leaving you feeling "drained."

2. ***Loss of Joy and Motivation***: When self-neglect becomes a pattern, activities that once brought you happiness or fulfillment may feel like burdens.

You may feel unmotivated, disconnected, or indifferent to things you used to enjoy. This loss of joy is often a sign that your emotional well-being is being neglected.

3. *Physical Symptoms*: Self-neglect can manifest in physical ways, such as frequent headaches, tension, digestive issues, or other ailments. These symptoms are your body's way of signaling that something is out of balance and needs attention.

4. *Irritability and Emotional Reactivity*: When you ignore your emotional needs, small inconveniences can feel overwhelming, and you may find yourself reacting strongly to minor issues. This is often a sign that unprocessed emotions are building up and need to be addressed.

5. **Difficulty Focusing or Making Decisions**: Mental neglect can lead to a sense of fogginess or indecisiveness, as your mind becomes cluttered and unfocused. This can make it hard to concentrate, remember details, or make thoughtful decisions.

6. *Isolation or Withdrawal*: Social neglect can lead to feelings of isolation and disconnection. You may avoid social interactions, withdraw from friends or family, or feel a sense of loneliness even when surrounded by others.

Recognizing these warning signs is a powerful step toward reclaiming your well-being. Each of these symptoms is a signal from your body and mind, a reminder that something needs your attention. Instead of pushing these feelings aside, use them as invitations to explore what might be missing or neglected in your life.

Why We Ignore the Signs

Despite the many signs, it's common to ignore or rationalize self-neglect. We convince ourselves that we're "too busy" to take care of ourselves, that our responsibilities are more important, or that self-care is selfish. Here are some common reasons why we ignore the signs of self-neglect:

1. *Cultural Conditioning*: Many cultures glorify self-sacrifice, productivity, and "grinding" as virtues. We're taught that working hard and putting others first is admirable, often at the expense of our own well-being. This mentality reinforces the idea that self-care is indulgent or secondary.

2. *Fear of Confrontation*: Acknowledging self-neglect requires us to confront uncomfortable truths about our choices, priorities, and beliefs. This introspection can be intimidating, so we avoid it, staying in our comfort zones instead.

3. *Guilt and Shame*: Self-neglect can also be driven by feelings of guilt or shame. We might feel guilty for prioritizing ourselves, thinking it's selfish or irresponsible. These feelings can prevent us from seeking the care and rest we need.

4. *Perfectionism*: The desire to appear strong and capable can lead us to push ourselves beyond our limits. We believe we should be able to handle *everything* on our own, leading us to ignore our needs in an attempt to maintain a facade of perfection.

5. *Numbing Behaviors*: Instead of addressing self-neglect, we may turn to numbing behaviors like overworking, binge-watching TV, or excessive scrolling on social media. These behaviors temporarily distract us but ultimately reinforce patterns of avoidance and neglect.

Understanding these tendencies is key to breaking the cycle of self-neglect. Recognize that prioritizing your well-being is not a sign of weakness or selfishness; it's an act of strength and self-respect.

Reclaiming Self-Care as a Necessity, Not a Luxury

Self-care is often misunderstood as a luxury, something we indulge in only when we have time. But in truth, self-care is a fundamental part of our well-being, a necessary act of self-respect that enables us to show up fully in our lives. Reclaiming self-care means redefining it as a priority, not an afterthought. Here are some steps to begin this process:

1. **Create Space for Self-Reflection**: Set aside time each day, even if it's just a few minutes, to check in with yourself. Use this time to journal, meditate, or simply reflect on how you're feeling and what you need.

2. **Set Boundaries with Compassion**: Boundaries are essential for protecting your energy and mental health. Practice saying no when you need to. Remember that setting boundaries is an act of kindness toward yourself and others.

3. **Identify Small Acts of Self-Care**: Self-care doesn't have to be elaborate or time-consuming. Small actions like going for a walk, drinking a glass of water, or taking a few deep breaths can make a significant difference.

4. **Prioritize Rest and Recovery**: Rest is not a reward; it's a necessity. Make sleep, relaxation, and downtime a regular part of your routine, and honor your body's need for recovery.

5. **Seek Support When Needed**: Remember that self-care doesn't have to be a solo journey. Reach out to friends, family, or professionals for support

when you need it. Allowing others to help you is an act of self-compassion.

Start small. Choose one thing—just one—that nourishes *you*. Then do it again tomorrow. Your healing is in the rhythm, not the rush.

Self-Care Truth: "I don't have to earn rest. I am allowed to care for myself simply because I exist."

Journal Reflection: Recognizing and Addressing Self-Neglect

As we close this chapter, take some time to reflect on your own patterns of self-neglect. Use the following questions to guide your journaling. Remember to be kind and honest with yourself as you explore these reflections.

1. What are the warning signs of self-neglect that I notice in myself?
2. Which areas of my life (physical, emotional, mental, social, spiritual) have I been neglecting?
3. Why have I been avoiding self-care, and what beliefs or fears might be contributing to this pattern?
4. What small act of self-care can I commit to this week?

5. Who can I reach out to for support, and how can I allow myself to accept help when needed?

These reflections are an opportunity to connect with yourself on a deeper level and to begin to rebuild a sense of care and respect for your needs. By acknowledging and addressing self-neglect, you're taking a vital step toward living a more balanced, fulfilling life that honors your whole self. In the next chapter, we'll explore how to reconnect with your purpose, helping you reclaim a sense of direction and meaning as you move forward on this journey.

"I may not have all the answers,
but I trust the wisdom within
me to guide the way."

CHAPTER 3

NAVIGATING WITH PURPOSE: RECLAIMING YOUR INNER COMPASS

"The answers you seek are within; quiet
the noise, trust your direction, and let
your inner compass lead you home."
—Quan Thomas

Rediscovering yourself isn't about finding something entirely new but reconnecting with something you already carry deep within your inner compass. This compass, your true north, is what intuitively guides you toward choices, people, and experiences that bring meaning, joy, and fulfillment to your life. Over time, though, many of us lose touch with this compass, being pulled in different directions by obligations, expectations, and the demands of daily life. Your inner compass is more than a collection of ideas or goals; it's the quiet voice that knows what feels right or wrong. The pull you feel toward certain dreams, and the sense of calm that settles in your heart when you honor your true values. Reconnecting with it doesn't happen overnight, and it can be difficult in a world that's constantly telling us who to be and what to want. But even if it's faint or buried beneath layers of self-doubt and external pressure, your compass is there, waiting to guide you back to yourself.

I ignored my inner compass for years—not because I didn't have it, but because I didn't trust it. I let other people's voices become louder than my own. But I remember one morning, sitting in silence with my journal, asking, 'What do I want? Like, truly want?' And for the first time in a long time, I didn't filter my answer. I didn't edit it to fit someone else's approval. I didn't shrink it to make others comfortable. I wrote what I *actually* wanted. Not what was expected. That one question cracked open a door I didn't know I had locked. Because your purpose doesn't shout—it whispers. And when you get still enough, it speaks

Why We Drift Away from Our Inner Compass

For most of us, this disconnection from our inner compass happens gradually. We start with an instinctual understanding of who we are and what feels right. But as we grow older, outside influences, society, family, and peers begin to shape our understanding of success, happiness, and fulfillment. Society offers us images of what a "successful" or "worthy" life looks like. It's often tied to material accomplishments, popularity, or external validation. Over time, we start measuring our worth by these external markers rather than our own sense of purpose and contentment.

For some, the expectations of family or culture can feel particularly powerful. Many of us inherit beliefs about what we "should" be doing or who we "should" become, making it difficult to prioritize our own values or aspirations. In trying to make others proud or fit into a specific mold, we may overlook our passions and interests, dismissing them as impractical or insignificant. This disconnection can lead us to a life that looks full on the outside but feels hollow inside.

Fear also plays a significant role. The fear of failing, disappointing others, or facing the unknown can keep us on safe, predictable paths that may not feel fulfilling. It's often easier to stick with what's familiar than listen to that quiet voice urging us to leap, even if it's toward something that could bring us true joy.

And then there's the simple act of busyness. Daily responsibilities, routines, and distractions fill up our time, leaving little room for self-reflection. The constant noise of email and text notifications pulls us outward. These demands make it difficult to hear the softer, deeper voice within. We might feel a nagging sense of emptiness or restlessness, but it's hard to pinpoint exactly what's wrong, and even harder to know where to begin.

The good news is that no matter how far you feel from your true self, it's never too late to reconnect. Your inner compass, that quiet yet steady guide, is always there, waiting to help you find your way back to what matters most.

Rediscovering What You Value

One of the first steps in reclaiming your inner compass is getting clear on what you value. What is important to you? Values are the principles that feel non-negotiable, the beliefs that bring meaning and direction to your life. When you live in alignment with your values, life feels harmonious and fulfilling. When you stray from them, even small decisions can feel disorienting or unsatisfying.

Think back to a time when you felt truly fulfilled or proud of yourself. What was it about that experience that felt meaningful? Maybe it was the sense of honesty in a conversation with a friend, the creativity you felt in a project, or the resilience you showed during a challenge. These moments often point to underlying values like connection, integrity, creativity, or growth that make life feel rich and purposeful.

On the flip side, consider moments that left you feeling uneasy or uncomfortable. Maybe you agreed to something that didn't feel right, or you stayed silent when you wanted to speak up. These experiences, too, reveal what you value by highlighting what doesn't sit well with you. If saying "yes" when you wanted to say "no" felt wrong, you might value authenticity or boundaries. If staying quiet left you uneasy, perhaps you value courage or self-expression.

Once you start to identify these values, try to hold them in your awareness as you go about your day. Let them act as guideposts, helping you make decisions and interact with the world in a way that feels true to who you are. This isn't about changing everything at once; it's about small, intentional choices that bring you closer to living in alignment with what matters to you.

This is for the person who has spent years putting themselves second. The person who's accomplished so much but still feels unfulfilled. The one who knows deep down they are meant for more—but hasn't been given permission to dream again.

Let this be your permission. You don't need a title, a degree, or anyone's approval to pursue what lights you up. What you feel pulling on your heart? That's not a coincidence. It's a calling.

Reigniting Passion and Purpose

Values give us direction, but passion is what fuels the journey. Passion is that unmistakable spark of joy, the excitement that lights you up from within. Yet, in the hustle and bustle of daily life, it's easy to let passion slip into the background, replaced by routine or practicality. Many of us end up following the path we think we "should" be on, only to realize later that we've sidelined what we truly care about.

So, how do you reconnect with your passions? Start by allowing yourself to be curious, become interested. Reigniting passion doesn't necessarily mean making big changes or turning your life upside down. It's about tuning in to what naturally brings you joy, excitement, or a sense of purpose. Sometimes, these passions are connected to childhood interests that have been put on hold—drawing, storytelling, helping others, building things, exploring the outdoors. Other times, they're related to activities or topics you've always wanted to try but haven't given yourself permission to pursue.

Begin with small steps. Pick up a book on a subject that fascinates you, take a weekend workshop, or set aside time each week for an activity that interests you. Think of it as an experiment rather than a commitment, giving yourself the freedom to explore without pressure. Pay attention to what energizes you, and what leaves you feeling alive and fulfilled. These are the moments when you're reconnecting with your true self, letting your inner compass guide you back to what matters most.

Listening to Your Intuition

Reclaiming your inner compass also involves learning to trust your intuition, the quiet, instinctual voice that knows what feels right. Intuition is that feeling in your gut, the subtle tug in a certain direction, or the sense of calm when you make a choice that aligns with your values. For many, though, intuition feels elusive or hard to recognize, especially if they've spent years ignoring or second-guessing it.

Start by giving your intuition space to speak. This might mean setting aside time each day for quiet reflection, whether through praying, meditation, journaling, or simply sitting in silence. The goal is to become comfortable with stillness so that you can tune in to the quieter signals within you. In a world that values logic and data, intuition might feel intangible or unreliable, but it's often our truest guide.

Begin to notice your physical responses to different situations. Your body often knows when something feels right or wrong, even before your mind catches up. Maybe you feel a sense of tension or unease when you consider a certain path, or maybe you feel a sense of lightness when you think about something else. Trusting these signals can help you make decisions that align with your inner compass, even if they don't make logical sense right away.

Here are some specific examples to tune into intuition:

1. **Observe Your Physical Reactions**: Your body often reacts instinctively. When faced with a decision, take a moment to notice any physical sensations. For example, if you feel a tightening in your chest at the thought of a new commitment, it may be your intuition signaling discomfort. Conversely, a feeling of lightness or excitement may indicate alignment.

2. **Ask Yourself "Yes" or "No" Questions**: Start by asking simple questions and observing your immediate reaction. For example, "Should I take this opportunity?" or "Am I excited about this project?" The first response is often the most honest, before logic intervenes.

3. **Identify Recurring Thoughts and Feelings**: Intuition often appears as a recurring thought or feeling. If you find yourself repeatedly drawn toward a certain path, or if a sense of unease arises around specific people or situations, pay attention. These patterns are your intuition's way of signaling alignment or misalignment.

4. **Allow Quiet Reflection**: Intuition thrives in stillness. Set aside time for silence through meditation, journaling, or a quiet walk. This space allows you to hear the quieter signals of intuition amidst daily noise.

Example: Imagine you're considering a career change but are unsure if it's the right move. By practicing these steps, you might notice excitement mixed with fear when you think about the new role. A consistent pull toward this change could indicate that, despite the uncertainty, it aligns with your deeper desires.

Remember, you don't have to make life-altering decisions based solely on intuition; instead, think of it as another layer of information that can guide you. By practicing listening to this inner voice in small, everyday choices, you build confidence in its guidance over time.

Realigning with Your Inner Compass

Reclaiming your inner compass isn't a single decision; it's a series of small choices made every day, an ongoing commitment to living in alignment with who you truly are. This journey requires patience, as well as a willingness to let go of the parts of your life that no longer resonate. Realigning with your inner compass isn't about changing everything all at once; it's about bringing more intention into your decisions, interactions, and daily routines.

Start by setting a daily intention to live in alignment with your values. Each morning, take a moment to reflect on one value that you want to bring into your day, whether it's compassion, courage, creativity, or balance. Let this value guide your actions, helping you navigate your day in a way that feels true to you.

Periodically, check in with yourself to see if you're on the right path. Life is constantly changing, and so are you, so this realignment is an ongoing process. Some days, it might feel easier than others, but the commitment to realignment is what keeps you connected to your inner compass, even when the world around you is noisy or demanding.

Be gentle with yourself along the way. This journey isn't about perfection; it's about making choices that bring you closer to your authentic self. There will be days when you feel out of alignment, and that's okay. What matters is that you continue to listen, reflect, and adjust, trusting that each step brings you closer to a life that feels true and fulfilling.

Compass Truth: "I trust my inner wisdom—even when the world doesn't understand it."

Start with one choice today that feels aligned. Say no when you mean no. Say yes to what brings peace. The more you trust your truth, the louder your compass will become.

Journal Exercise: Reclaiming Your Inner Compass

Take a few moments to reflect on where you are in relation to your inner compass. Use the questions below to guide your journaling, allowing yourself to explore without judgment. These reflections are not about finding definitive answers; they're about reconnecting with yourself and making space for whatever comes up.

1. What values feel most important to me right now, and how am I honoring them in my daily life?
2. When do I feel most alive, connected, or fulfilled? What activities or moments make me feel this way?
3. How can I begin to trust my intuition more? What small steps can I take to let it guide my choices?
4. What areas of my life feel out of alignment, and how can I gently realign them with my values?
5. In what small ways can I create space for my passions, even amidst my responsibilities and routines?

Each question is an invitation to connect with your inner compass, to listen to the parts of you that know what feels true. The journey to reclaiming this compass is ongoing, a path that may twist and turn but ultimately lead you closer to the person you're meant to be. In the next chapter, we'll explore the importance of self-image and self-worth, two pillars that play a powerful role in building a life of authenticity, resilience, and fulfillment.

"My worth is not up for debate.
I am enough exactly as I am."

CHAPTER 4

UNCOVERING YOUR INNER WORTH

"You are not a reflection of what you've
achieved or what others think of you.
You are a reflection of how deeply you
honor your own worth and embrace
the person you're becoming."
—Quan Thomas

Self-worth is the deep-rooted belief that we are valuable just as we are, while self-image is how we view ourselves, our strengths, flaws, and potential. When self-worth and self-image are strong and aligned, they create a foundation that supports us through challenges, enabling us to grow, take risks, and pursue fulfillment. I want to invite you to reimagine self-worth as intrinsic and self-image as a flexible, supportive force that helps you see yourself with compassion, courage, and confidence.

We live in a society that often measures worth by achievements, appearances, or status. These standards can make self-worth feel conditional and fragile, as if it depends on constantly proving ourselves. But real self-worth isn't earned or given; it's an inner state that exists within each of us, regardless of what we accomplish. There was a time when I thought I had to *do more* to be worth more. That the more I achieved, the more I deserved love, peace, or rest.

But the moment that changed me wasn't during a big success—it was after a quiet failure. Something didn't go the way I planned, and instead of spiraling into self-criticism like I usually did, I stopped. I looked in the mirror and said, 'You're still worthy.' Not because I crushed it. Not because I proved anything. Just because I am. That simple sentence felt radical. I said it again. And again. Until I believed it. That was the moment I began to love myself for *being*, not just doing.

It is important that we learn to uncover that inner sense of worth, understanding how to quiet the voice of self-criticism, and reshaping our self-image to reflect a more compassionate, resilient version of ourselves. Embracing these changes can be empowering, helping us face life with renewed confidence and joy.

Moving Beyond Conditional Self-Worth

One of the most common yet subtle traps is the idea of conditional self-worth, the belief that we are valuable only if we achieve certain things, meet others' expectations, or succeed according to society's standards. Having this mindset often develops in childhood, reinforced by praise when we perform well or succeed. Over time, we may begin to equate our value with what we accomplish rather than who we are, creating a sense that our worth depends on what we do rather than simply being enough as we are.

Think about it this way: imagine trying to fill a bucket with a hole in the bottom. No matter how much you pour into it, it will never be full. That's the reality of conditional self-worth. Even if we reach a goal or receive praise, the satisfaction is temporary because it doesn't come from a place of inner fulfillment. It's exhausting, as we constantly chase the next achievement, hoping it will finally make us feel worthy, but it rarely does.

To move beyond conditional self-worth, begin by recognizing moments when you base your value on external factors. Ask yourself if you are pursuing certain goals to genuinely fulfill yourself, or if they're driven by a need for validation. Shifting from external validation to inner fulfillment takes time, but it's powerful. Imagine the freedom of knowing that your worth is secure, unshaken by failures or setbacks. This doesn't mean giving up on goals or ambitions; rather, it means pursuing them from a place of love for yourself, not from a need to prove yourself.

A daily affirmation can be helpful: **"My worth is not tied to what I achieve. I am enough, just as I am."** Repeat this to yourself, especially in moments of self-doubt. Over time, this shift in perspective can change how you see yourself and help you approach your dreams and challenges with confidence, knowing that your worth is unshakeable.

Redefining Your Self-Image

Our self-image is the mental picture we carry of ourselves, shaped by the stories we tell ourselves about who we are, what we're capable of, and what we deserve. This picture is often influenced by past experiences, feedback from others, and cultural expectations. Unfortunately, many of us carry self-images rooted in outdated stories or past hurts, limiting our ability to grow, heal, and explore new possibilities.

Imagine that your self-image is like a photograph you've been holding onto for years. Over time, this photograph might become faded, distorted, or inaccurate. The person you are today may no longer match that old picture, yet you still see yourself through that lens. If you've been holding onto beliefs like "I'm not capable," "I'm too sensitive," or "I always fall short," it's time to challenge and rewrite these stories.

Start by reflecting on moments when you surprised yourself, times when you showed resilience, tried something new, or pushed through a challenge. These moments offer clues about who you truly are beyond any limiting beliefs. Your self-image is not static; it can change, evolve, and grow. As you build a new self-image, focus on your strengths, resilience, and potential. Allow yourself to be curious and open, realizing that the person you're becoming is dynamic, full of potential, and worthy of compassion.

Visualize the self-image you want to carry forward—an image rooted in possibility, not limitation. See yourself as someone who is resilient, capable, and worthy. When doubts arise, remember that old images don't define you. With each new day and each small act of courage, you are reshaping your self-image and allowing yourself to become a truer, stronger version of who you are.

Close your eyes and picture the version of yourself you're becoming—the version that knows your worth, sets boundaries, and walks with quiet confidence.

What does he/she look like? How does he/she talk to herself?

Now—start showing up for *YOU.* Speak to yourself the way he/she would. Make decisions the way he/she would. Every time you choose yourself over your old story, you rewrite your self-image in real time.

Practicing Self-Compassion

Self-compassion is the bridge that connects self-worth and self-image. It's the practice of treating yourself with kindness, understanding, and forgiveness, especially during times of struggle or disappointment. Many of us have an internal voice that's quick to criticize, judge, and point out our shortcomings. This inner critic, while sometimes well-intentioned, often causes more harm than good, trapping us in cycles of shame and self-doubt.]

Think of self-compassion as the voice of a caring friend. When we make a mistake, fall short, or face a setback, a compassionate friend would offer understanding and support, not harsh judgment. Self-compassion allows us to show ourselves the same kindness, softening our approach to challenges and mistakes. This practice doesn't mean ignoring areas for growth or avoiding accountability; it means recognizing that growth is a journey, and mistakes are a natural part of it.

Next time you catch yourself being self-critical, pause and ask, "How would I speak to a friend in this situation?" Then, try to apply that same kindness to yourself. You might say, "I'm doing the best I can, and it's okay to make mistakes," or "I'm learning and growing, and that takes time." With practice, self-compassion becomes a source of strength, helping you approach challenges with resilience and a greater sense of inner peace.

Self-compassion isn't just about comfort; it's also about motivation. People who are kind to themselves are often more resilient, more willing to try new things, and less likely to give up in the face of setbacks. By being gentle with yourself, you're not only nurturing self-worth but also creating a supportive environment for growth and transformation.

Letting Go of Perfectionism

Perfectionism is a common struggle that can undermine self-worth and self-image. It's the belief that we must be flawless to be valuable, loved, or successful. While aiming for high standards can be motivating, perfectionism creates an impossible standard. When we expect ourselves to be perfect, we become hyper-aware of every flaw, mistake, or shortcoming, leading to a constant feeling of inadequacy.

Letting go of perfectionism involves shifting from a mindset of "I must be perfect" to "I am enough as I am." Recognize that perfection is an illusion, a standard that nobody can meet. Instead of perfection, aim for progress. Focus on doing your best, celebrating small steps, and learning from mistakes. This approach creates space for growth, resilience, and enjoyment, allowing you to pursue goals without the burden of unrealistic expectations.

Think about a recent project, goal, or relationship where you felt pressure to be perfect. Now imagine approaching it with a mindset of curiosity rather than pressure. What would change if you allowed yourself to try, experiment, and learn without fear of falling short? By embracing imperfection, you're freeing yourself to take risks, explore your interests, and experience life without the constant weight of self-criticism.

A helpful mantra to remind yourself might be, "I strive for progress, not perfection." Repeat this when you feel the urge to overanalyze, criticize, or hold yourself to impossible standards. This shift in perspective can be liberating, helping you pursue your passions, build meaningful relationships, and embrace life with authenticity and joy.

Releasing Comparison and Embracing Your Own Path

Comparison can be a significant obstacle to self-worth, especially in today's world of social media and curated images. We see others' successes, relationships, and achievements, and it's easy to feel like we're falling short. This constant comparison can drain our energy and leave us feeling disconnected from our own unique journey.

To move beyond comparison, start by focusing on gratitude and personal growth. Reflect on the qualities, experiences, and strengths that make your journey unique. What are you proud of? What have you overcome? By recognizing your own progress and celebrating who you are, you shift the focus from what others are doing to the meaningful path you're on.

Consider writing a list of qualities and accomplishments that are meaningful to you. This practice can help you reconnect with your own values and achievements, reinforcing a sense of gratitude and self-worth. When you feel the pull of comparison, remind yourself that everyone's journey is different, with its own challenges, setbacks, and triumphs. Your worth is not defined by how you measure up to others—but by your own values, progress, and resilience.

A helpful exercise when comparison arises is to pause and redirect your energy toward gratitude. Think of one thing about yourself, your life, or your path that you're grateful for. This simple shift in focus can help ground you in the present, reminding you that your journey is unique and valuable and that it's worth celebrating.

Affirming Self-Worth and Building a Positive Self-Image

Building a foundation of self-worth and a supportive self-image is an ongoing practice. One way to reinforce these beliefs is through daily affirmations. Affirmations are positive statements that help you internalize empowering beliefs. When repeated consistently, they can reshape your mindset, counteract negative self-talk, and nurture a more positive self-image.

Choose a few affirmations that resonate deeply with you, such as:

> "I am worthy of love and respect,"
> "I am enough just as I am,"
> "I am capable of growth and change."

Say these affirmations daily, either in the morning to start your day with positivity or in the evening as a reflection practice. With time, these affirmations become more than just words; they become reminders of your inner strength and worth, helping you cultivate a self-image that reflects who you truly are.

Affirmations also work best when paired with small, intentional actions. For example, if your affirmation is "I am capable of growth and change," look for small ways to stretch yourself whether it's learning a new skill, practicing patience, or taking on a new challenge. Each time you follow through, you reinforce your belief in your own capabilities, helping to shift your self-image from doubt to confidence.

Worthiness Truth: "My value is not up for negotiation. I am worthy—without performance, permission, or perfection."

Self-worth doesn't begin in others' eyes—it begins in how you *look at yourself.*

Journal Exercise: Redefining Self-Worth and Self-Image

To deepen your understanding of self-worth and self-image, take some time to reflect on these questions in your journal:

1. How do I define my self-worth, and are there conditions I place on feeling worthy?
2. What beliefs about myself feel limiting, and how can I start reframing them?
3. What qualities do I appreciate about myself, beyond achievements or appearances?
4. How does perfectionism affect me, and what would it feel like to let go of it?
5. What unique strengths or experiences make my journey valuable and meaningful?

By exploring these questions, you are beginning the work of redefining self-worth and self-image. Embracing your own journey, letting go of comparison, and choosing self-compassion are powerful steps toward becoming the truest, most resilient version of yourself. In the next chapter, we'll explore how resilience can help you overcome life's challenges with strength and clarity, bringing you closer to a life that reflects your values and passions.

"Even in my hardest moments, I rise with strength, grace, and faith."

CHAPTER 5

BUILDING RESILIENCE THROUGH CHALLENGES

"Strength doesn't come from avoiding
struggles; it comes from embracing
them and finding the courage to
grow through each challenge."
—Quan Thomas

Resilience is a foundational quality that allows us to face life's inevitable challenges with strength, flexibility, and hope. Resilience, however, doesn't mean continuing to deal with adversity and doing nothing about it. It also doesn't mean avoiding hardship or never feeling pain; it means finding the courage to move forward even when the path is difficult. It's the capacity to adapt, to learn, and to bounce back from setbacks. Many people think of resilience as a trait you're either born with or without, but in truth, resilience is a skill that can be developed and strengthened over time. I didn't learn resilience in comfort—I learned it in chaos. There was a season when everything felt like it was falling apart—personally, emotionally, spiritually. I kept trying to hold it all together. I prayed. I pushed. I smiled through tears. But it wasn't until I let myself fall apart that I found strength I didn't know I had. I remember sitting on the edge of my bed, whispering to God, 'I don't know what to do. I don't even know who I am right now.' And in the silence, I heard it: *Start again. But this time, start with you.*

That moment didn't change my circumstances overnight—but it changed my posture. I stopped performing strength and started practicing surrender. That's when my real resilience was born.

By understanding the mindsets and habits that foster resilience, you can equip yourself with tools to face life's difficulties with courage, empowering you to not only endure but to grow through adversity. We have to embrace resilience as a pathway to self-trust, confidence, and self-compassion, helping you weather life's storms and emerge stronger and wiser.

Understanding Resilience: What It Is and What It Isn't

Resilience is often misunderstood as being tough or stoic in the face of adversity. However, true resilience isn't about suppressing emotions or pretending everything is fine. In fact, resilient people are those who are willing to feel their emotions, acknowledge their struggles, and take action toward healing. Resilience is about finding balance—it's the ability to experience pain, disappointment, or uncertainty and still hold onto hope, adapting and adjusting as you go.

Imagine resilience as a tree that bends with the wind instead of breaking. Just as a tree's roots anchor it firmly in the ground, your values, sense of purpose, and inner strength help you remain grounded. The tree's branches may sway, but its roots keep it steady. Similarly, resilience allows you to stay anchored in your values and purpose, even as life's challenges push and pull you in different directions.

Resilience is not about denying difficulty but about learning to navigate it. This means honoring both your strength and your vulnerability, knowing that resilience is not a single trait but a collection of qualities, such as patience, flexibility, courage, and hope—that altogether allow you to adapt and grow. Embracing resilience in this way can be liberating, as it frees you from the need to "have it all together" and instead invites you to show up authentically, with all your strengths and imperfections.

The Benefits of Resilience

Resilience is not just about surviving difficult times; it's about finding ways to thrive through them. When you build resilience, you develop a mindset that helps you face obstacles without losing sight of your goals. Here are some of the profound benefits that resilience brings:

Emotional Stability: Resilient people are better able to manage their emotions during challenging times. They experience feelings of sadness, frustration, or fear, but they don't allow these emotions to control their actions. Instead, they acknowledge them, find healthy ways to cope, and stay committed to moving forward.

Adaptability: Life rarely goes as planned, and resilience helps you adapt to unexpected changes. Rather than resisting or fearing change, resilient people learn to see it as an opportunity for growth. This adaptability makes it easier to navigate new situations, embrace learning experiences, and remain open to possibilities.

Increased Self-Confidence: Resilience builds self-trust. Each time you overcome a challenge, you reinforce your belief in your own strength and capability. This confidence spills over into other areas of life, empowering you to take risks, pursue your goals, and believe in your potential.

A Sense of Purpose: When you view challenges as part of a greater journey, resilience gives you a sense of purpose. Instead of feeling defeated by hardship, resilient people often see it as a meaningful part of life's unfolding, a lesson that contributes to their growth.

Resilience isn't about eliminating difficulty, but it does transform how you respond to it. When you view challenges as part of your journey, they become less intimidating and more manageable. Instead of "must survive," categorize challenges as opportunities to deepen your understanding, refine your goals, and grow in self-trust.

There's power in knowing that your pain is not wasted. God never promised we wouldn't face storms— He promised we wouldn't face them alone. Resilience isn't about being unshaken; it's about knowing where your strength comes from when you are. Every setback you've survived is evidence of grace. Every time you got back up, even if it was messy—that was divine resilience at work.

Developing a Resilient Mindset

Building resilience starts with cultivating a resilient mindset. This does not include rigid positivity or denying hardships. A resilient mindset learns to view setbacks as temporary and as opportunities for growth. It helps you keep perspective, focusing on what you can control and letting go of what you can't.

One of the foundations of a resilient mindset is self-compassion. Rather than criticizing yourself when things don't go as planned, self-compassion allows you to acknowledge your pain, understand that struggle is a universal human experience, and respond with kindness.

Self-compassion is critical in difficult times because it allows you to be honest about your feelings without judgment. This honesty, in turn, helps you process your emotions in a healthy way, which is essential for resilience.

Flexibility is an equally important part of a resilient mindset. Life is full of uncertainties, and the ability to adapt is a cornerstone of resilience. When you face a setback, ask yourself, "How can I approach this differently?" Instead of viewing a single failure as an end, see it as a prompt to explore new paths, make adjustments, and try again. Flexibility doesn't mean giving up on your goals; it means remaining open to the idea that there may be different, even better, ways to reach them.

Embracing Vulnerability as a Strength

In our culture, vulnerability is often seen as a weakness, something to hide or avoid. But vulnerability is one of the greatest sources of resilience. When you allow yourself to be vulnerable, you open up to connection, support, and learning. Vulnerability means admitting that you're struggling, and being honest about your needs allows others to support you. It reminds you that you don't have to face challenges alone.

Showing yourself vulnerable also gives you permission to acknowledge and feel your emotions. Resilient people are not those who push down their feelings; they're the ones who experience and express them without shame. They understand that sadness, frustration, and even anger are natural responses to hardship, and they process these feelings in healthy ways.Think about times when you've allowed yourself to be vulnerable. Maybe you shared a fear with a friend, sought help from someone you trust, or admitted to yourself that you were struggling. In these moments, vulnerability likely felt uncomfortable yet relieving, creating a space for healing and resilience. Embracing vulnerability doesn't weaken you; it strengthens your ability to cope, connect, and grow through life's challenges.

Building Resilience through Daily Practices

Just as physical strength is built through consistent exercise, resilience is built through small, daily practices that reinforce mental and emotional strength. Here are some ways to integrate resilience-building habits into your daily life:

Mindfulness: Mindfulness is staying present and fully engaged in the moment, without judgment. Practicing mindfulness can help you stay calm in the face of challenges, as it encourages you to focus on what you can control and let go of worry. Simple practices like deep breathing, grounding exercises, or a few minutes of meditation each day can help build resilience by strengthening your ability to stay centered, even during stressful times.

Journaling: Journaling is a powerful tool for processing emotions, reflecting on challenges, and gaining insight into your thoughts and behaviors. Take time each day or week to write about your experiences, especially during difficult times. This can help you make sense of setbacks, identify patterns, and develop a clearer perspective on how to move forward.

Self-Care: Resilience isn't just mental; it's also physical. Taking care of your body with enough rest, nutrition, and exercise is essential to maintaining your strength during difficult times. Self-care also means setting boundaries, saying no when necessary, and making space for relaxation and joy. When you feel physically well, you're better equipped to handle emotional challenges with resilience.

Seeking Support: Resilient people know they don't have to face challenges alone. Build a support system of friends, family members, or mentors who can provide encouragement, guidance, and understanding. Reaching out for support is not a sign of weakness; it's a strength that reinforces resilience by reminding you that you're not alone.

By making these practices part of your routine, you gradually build a foundation of resilience that strengthens over time. These habits create a strong, supportive environment that helps you cope with challenges, heal from setbacks, and keep you moving forward.

Finding Meaning in Hardship

One of the most powerful aspects of resilience is the ability to find meaning in hardship. When life throws us a curveball, it's natural to feel discouraged, frustrated, or overwhelmed. But resilient people often view challenges as opportunities to learn, grow, and strengthen their character. They ask, "What can I learn from this?" or "How might this experience help me grow?"

Finding meaning doesn't mean downplaying the pain of difficult experiences. It means acknowledging the challenge while seeking lessons or insights that can help you become a better, more resilient person. This mindset can transform adversity into a stepping stone, helping you develop patience, empathy, and courage.

Reflect on past challenges that taught you valuable lessons or helped you become more compassionate or understanding. By recognizing the growth from these experiences, you begin to fear hardship less and instead see it as a meaningful part of your journey. This perspective builds resilience and deepens your appreciation for the strength and wisdom you've developed through life's challenges.

Resilience Truth: "I am not defined by what tried to break me. I am refined by what built me back stronger."

You don't need to have it all together. You just need to keep going with grace.

Journal Exercise: Cultivating Resilience

To close this chapter, take a moment to reflect on your resilience. Use these questions as journaling prompts or points of introspection:

1. How do I typically respond to challenges, and what does this reveal about my current level of resilience?
2. What small practices can I incorporate into my life to strengthen my resilience?
3. In what ways have past challenges helped me grow, and how can I use these lessons to face future difficulties?
4. Who are the people in my life who support my resilience, and how can I reach out to them during challenging times?
5. What personal values or beliefs keep me anchored during adversity, and how can I lean into these values in moments of difficulty?

These reflections are a way to honor your resilience and identify areas for growth. Resilience does not make us immune to struggle; it builds our strength to face it with grace, courage, and hope. By developing resilience, you're equipping yourself with a toolset that empowers you to handle life's challenges with greater ease; helping you navigate the storms and the calm with a sense of purpose and trust in yourself. In the next chapter, we'll delve into the role of self-discovery and how embracing your unique qualities can further enrich your journey of growth.

**"I release the need to perform
and embrace the freedom
of being fully me."**

CHAPTER 6

UNCOVERING YOUR AUTHENTIC SELF

"The journey to authenticity is
a path inward; only by knowing
and embracing who you truly are
can you shine in the world."
—Quan Thomas

In a world full of expectations, opinions, and societal pressures, discovering who you truly are can feel exhilarating and challenging. Self-discovery is the process of exploring your unique qualities, desires, beliefs, and passions. It's a journey that leads you closer to your authentic self, the version of you that exists beyond the roles you play, the responsibilities you carry, and the expectations you feel compelled to meet. Embracing self-discovery is about uncovering what makes you unique, what drives you, and what truly brings you joy and fulfillment.

Self-discovery is more than just introspection; it's connecting with your true self in a way that feels real and empowering. Many people live their lives on autopilot, caught up in routines and habits that may not reflect who they truly are. But discovering your authentic self opens doors to new possibilities, deeper relationships, and a stronger sense of purpose.

I'll never forget the moment I reconnected with a part of myself I thought was gone. I was cleaning and found an old journal I had written in years ago. Inside were pages of dreams, affirmations and prayers. I had completely forgotten that version of me existed—the one who believed, created, imagined. I sat there and cried—not out of sadness, but relief. Because she was still in me. Buried, quieted... but not gone. That's when I realized: ***the authentic you doesn't need to be created—they just need to be remembered.***

Why Self-Discovery Matters

Self-discovery is foundational to living an authentic, fulfilling life. When you know who you are and what you stand for, you make choices that align with your values and bring you closer to your goals. Without self-discovery, it's easy to get swept up in the opinions of others, following paths that may look good on the surface but leave you unfulfilled or disconnected.

Think of self-discovery as a compass. Knowing your true self gives you an inner guide that helps you navigate life's complexities with clarity and confidence. You're better equipped to set boundaries, pursue meaningful goals, and build nourishing relationships. Knowing yourself also allows you to show up authentically in the world, attracting people and opportunities that resonate with who you truly are.

At its core, self-discovery is an act of self-love and self-respect. By dedicating time and energy to understanding yourself, you acknowledge your worth and recognize that your happiness and fulfillment are important. Self-discovery empowers you to live a life that is uniquely yours, free from the constraints of other people's expectations.

Starting with Curiosity

The journey of self-discovery begins with curiosity. Imagine approaching yourself as if you were meeting a fascinating person for the first time, someone you genuinely want to understand. Cultivating curiosity allows you to explore your thoughts, feelings, and behaviors without judgment. Instead of criticizing yourself or feeling the need to fit into predefined molds, curiosity permits you to be open, to question, and to embrace your uniqueness.

Begin asking yourself questions that invite reflection and exploration. Here are a few prompts to help you get started:

What brings me joy? Reflect on the activities, people, and experiences that genuinely make you feel alive. Joy is often a powerful indicator of what aligns with your true self.

What values guide my decisions? Think about the principles that feel non-negotiable to you: honesty, compassion, creativity, and growth. These values are like signposts that point you toward a life that feels meaningful and fulfilling.

What are my natural strengths and talents? Acknowledging your strengths isn't about pride; it's about recognizing what you have to offer and how you can make a positive impact.

What experiences have been the most defining in my life? Reflecting on meaningful moments or turning points can reveal important insights into your character, resilience, and passions.

These questions aren't about finding definitive answers. They are meant to spark curiosity and open the door to deeper understanding. Self-discovery is a process, not a destination, and curiosity keeps you engaged, allowing you to continue learning and growing.

Letting Go of Roles and Labels

One of the biggest obstacles to self-discovery is the tendency to define ourselves by the roles we play or the labels we carry. Many of us go through life identifying ourselves by our careers, family roles, or social identities. While these aspects are a part of us, they don't define us completely. If we become overly attached to these roles, it can be difficult to see ourselves outside of them, leading us to lose touch with our authentic self.

Imagine peeling away each role or label, like layers of an onion. Beneath the surface, there's a part of you that exists beyond any single identity—a part that is constant and true. Take time to explore who you are without these labels. What are your interests, dreams, and values outside of the roles you play? What qualities define you when you're simply being, without the pressures to perform or fulfill others' expectations?

This exercise can feel liberating and uncomfortable. It may raise questions about what you truly want in life, which might differ from what you've been pursuing. But letting go of roles and labels is an essential part of self-discovery. It allows you to connect with a more authentic version of yourself and make choices based on your true desires.

If you've ever said, 'I don't even know who I am anymore,' you're not alone. You've worn the titles. You've kept the peace. You've done what was expected. But hear me when I say this: *You were never meant to live your whole life performing for approval*. The real you— the whole you—is allowed to exist beyond productivity, people-pleasing, and pretending.

Embracing Your Unique Qualities

We live in a world that often celebrates conformity, which can make us feel as if we need to fit a specific mold to be accepted or successful. But self-discovery is about embracing what makes you unique, even if it doesn't align with societal norms or expectations. Your quirks, talents, and perspectives are all parts of your authentic self, and they deserve to be honored.

Consider what makes you different. Perhaps you have a unique sense of humor, a knack for empathy, or an unconventional way of thinking. These qualities are gifts, and embracing them allows you to show up in the world in a way that's true to you. Self-discovery isn't about molding yourself to fit in; it's celebrating the parts of you that stand out, even if they don't fit the traditional definition of "success."

Start by practicing self-acceptance. Instead of viewing your differences as flaws, see them as strengths that make you who you are. Remind yourself that authenticity is a gift to yourself and others. When you embrace your uniqueness, you inspire others to do the same, creating a ripple effect that encourages authenticity and acceptance in the world around you.

Exploring Your Passions and Interests

Passions are a window into your true self. They're the activities, topics, or causes that ignite a spark within you and make life feel vibrant. But sometimes, life's demands can cause us to lose touch with these passions, especially if they don't seem "productive" or practical. Embracing self-discovery involves reconnecting with what excites you and finding ways to incorporate it into your life.

Ask yourself what you would do if time and resources were unlimited. What would you pursue, simply for the joy of it? Whether it's writing, painting, helping others, or exploring nature, these passions reflect a core part of who you are. They don't have to be career-related or lead to financial gain; their value lies in how they make you feel and the fulfillment they bring.

To start exploring your passions, make a list of activities you've always wanted to try or hobbies you used to enjoy but may have set aside. Choose one to incorporate back into your life, even if it's in a small way. For example, if you love painting but haven't done it in years, set aside an hour each week to paint. By nurturing your passions, you create space for joy and self-expression, which are essential to self-discovery.

Reflecting on Past Experiences and Lessons

Our past experiences often hold valuable insights into who we are and what we value. By reflecting on the positive and challenging moments in your life, you can gain a deeper understanding of your strengths, patterns, and growth areas. Self-discovery is not just about looking forward; it's also about learning from where you've been.

Think back to moments when you felt proud, fulfilled, or at peace. What were you doing? Who were you with? These memories can reveal aspects of yourself that you may want to nurture or bring into your life more fully. Likewise, consider the challenges you've faced. What did these experiences teach you? How did they shape your values, resilience, and perspective?

Reflection allows you to see your life as a journey, with each experience adding to your understanding of yourself. By embracing the joys and the lessons of the past, you cultivate a sense of self-awareness that supports your growth. This awareness also helps you let go of regrets and appreciate the path that has led you to where you are today.

Honoring Your Inner Voice

In a world that's often filled with noise and opinions, honoring your inner voice is essential to self-discovery. Your inner voice is that quiet sense of "knowing" that resides within you, guiding you toward choices that feel true and align with who you are. Listening to this voice requires mindfulness, patience, and trust.

Practice tuning in to your inner voice by spending time in silence, journaling, or engaging in activities that allow you to connect with yourself. Notice when your intuition speaks up, especially in situations where something doesn't feel right, or conversely, when something feels exciting and meaningful. Your inner voice is a valuable guide, often pointing you toward paths that align with your authentic self, even if they don't make logical sense.

Learning to trust your inner voice can take time, especially if you're used to relying on external opinions or validation. But the more you practice listening to it, the stronger and clearer it becomes. Your inner voice is a reflection of your true self, and honoring it is a powerful step in the journey of self-discovery.

Identity Truth: "I am not who the world told me to be. I am who God designed me to remember."

Let this be the season where you stop auditioning for acceptance and start embracing your wholeness.

Journal Exercise: Embracing Self-Discovery

To deepen your journey of self-discovery, take time to reflect on these questions. Use them as journaling prompts, allowing yourself to explore your answers without judgment or expectation.

1. What makes me feel most alive, joyful, or fulfilled?
2. How do my values influence my choices, and are there ways I can fully honor them?
3. What unique qualities do I bring to my relationships and experiences, and how can I openly embrace them?
4. Which past experiences have shaped who I am, and what lessons have they taught me?
5. When I listen to my inner voice, what does it tell me about my path, my desires, or my true self?

These reflections are an invitation to connect with yourself on a deeper level and uncover the qualities and values that make you uniquely you. The journey of self-discovery is ongoing, filled with twists, surprises, and insights that deepen your understanding of who you are. As you embrace this journey, remember that self-discovery is not about reaching a final destination; it's about honoring the process of becoming, allowing yourself to grow, explore, and evolve as you build a life that feels authentic and fulfilling.

In the next chapter, we'll explore how setting boundaries and honoring your needs can further support your growth, allowing you to cultivate a life of balance, joy, and self-respect.

"My life reflects what matters most to me—peace, truth, and alignment."

CHAPTER 7

SETTING BOUNDARIES AND HONORING YOUR NEEDS

"Boundaries are the space where
self-respect and compassion
for others coexist."
—Quan Thomas

Two empowering yet difficult steps toward personal growth are learning to set boundaries and honoring your own needs. Boundaries are the limits you establish to protect your well-being, time, and energy. They allow you to show up as your best self in your relationships, work, and personal pursuits. Honoring your needs involves recognizing what you require to feel balanced, healthy, and fulfilled. It also involves taking action to meet those needs without guilt or hesitation. Setting boundaries can feel uncomfortable at first, especially if you've been conditioned to put others' needs before your own. Often, we are taught that saying "no" is selfish or taking time for ourselves can damage relationships. But boundaries are not walls or barriers; they're guidelines that create space for respect and authenticity. They communicate your values and prioritize your well-being, ensuring that you can give to others from a place of wholeness rather than depletion. Honoring your needs and setting boundaries are acts of self-love that allow you to live a more intentional, balanced life.

Why Boundaries Matter

Boundaries are essential because they protect your energy and well-being, helping you maintain a sense of balance and fulfillment. When we don't set boundaries, it's easy to become overwhelmed, exhausted, or resentful. Without boundaries, we might say "yes" to things we don't have the time or energy for, allowing ourselves to be pulled in too many directions and struggling to find time for our own needs and goals.

Imagine your personal energy as a reservoir. Each interaction, commitment, and responsibility you take on draws from this reservoir. Without boundaries, it's easy to find yourself running on empty, with little energy left for the things that truly matter. Boundaries allow you to manage this energy, prioritizing what aligns with your values and letting go of what doesn't. When you have healthy boundaries, you can give and contribute in ways that feel fulfilling rather than draining.

Boundaries also create healthier relationships. When you communicate your limits clearly and respectfully, you encourage others to do the same, fostering a sense of mutual respect and understanding. Setting boundaries doesn't mean you care any less about others; it means you respect both yourself and them enough to create a relationship rooted in honesty and integrity. By prioritizing boundaries, you're not only protecting your well-being but also setting an example of self-respect that others can appreciate and emulate.

Identifying Your Needs

Before you can set effective boundaries, it's essential to understand your own needs. Needs are the things that sustain you emotionally, mentally, physically, and spiritually. They're the elements of life that help you feel balanced, supported, and at peace. Honoring your needs doesn't make you selfish; it's an essential part of self-care that enables you to thrive.

Start by reflecting on what you need to feel well. These needs might include things like time alone, physical exercise, creative expression, or emotional connection with loved ones. Consider your daily routines and commitments. Are they structured in a way that honors your needs, or do they often leave you feeling depleted? Identifying your needs requires honest self-reflection, acknowledging where you might be neglecting yourself and recognizing what brings you a sense of balance.

It's also helpful to tune into your emotions as a guide for identifying unmet needs. Feelings of resentment, frustration, or exhaustion often indicate areas where you're overextending yourself or not honoring your boundaries. For example, if you feel resentful about a work commitment, it might be a sign that you need more personal time or that your workload is unsustainable. By listening to these emotional cues, you can gain clarity on the boundaries you need to set to create a life that aligns with your well-being.

Types of Boundaries and How to Set Them

If you have been struggling with setting boundaries you are not alone. Setting boundaries helps protect your well-being by creating limits that honor your values and priorities. Boundaries can take various forms, depending on the needs they address. Here are examples of different types of boundaries and practical ways to set them in everyday situations.

1. **Physical Boundaries**: Physical boundaries protect your personal space and physical well-being. They relate to how you allow others to interact with

you physically and the space you need to feel comfortable.

Example in Practice: Suppose you have a friend who tends to invade your personal space, making you uncomfortable. You could kindly say, "I'd appreciate it if we could maintain a little more space when we talk. It helps me feel more comfortable." This approach respects both your need for space and the relationship, without sounding confrontational.

In the Workplace: If a colleague frequently approaches your desk without notice, a physical boundary might involve letting them know, "I prefer if we schedule time to discuss things instead of unexpected drop-ins." This boundary creates a more comfortable work environment and respects your need for focus.

2. **Emotional Boundaries**: Emotional boundaries involve protecting your emotional well-being. They help manage the emotional demands others place on you and allow you to safeguard your feelings, especially in emotionally charged situations.
   Example in Practice: If a friend often shares distressing stories that leave you feeling drained, you might gently set an emotional boundary by saying, "I care about you, but sometimes these

stories affect me deeply. Could we balance our conversations with lighter topics too?" This approach allows you to be present for your friend while prioritizing your emotional health.

In Relationships: In close relationships, emotional boundaries might look like letting a partner know, "I need a little time to process my feelings before we discuss things." This boundary allows you to address conflicts with clarity, reducing emotional overwhelm.

3. **Time Boundaries**:

Time boundaries help you manage how you allocate your time and energy, preventing others from monopolizing your schedule. They ensure that you have time for self-care, work, and other personal commitments.

Example in Practice: If a coworker frequently asks you to stay late or take on extra tasks, you could set a time boundary by saying, "I can help with this project, but I'll need to leave by 5 p.m." This sets a clear limit, respecting both your professional and personal time.

With Friends or Family: Suppose a friend wants to meet often, but you need some downtime to recharge. You might say, "I'd love to spend time with you, but I can only meet once a week." This time boundary maintains the relationship without compromising your need for rest.

Learning to Say "No" with Confidence

One of the most powerful tools in setting boundaries is the ability to say "no" with confidence and without guilt. For many, saying "no" feels uncomfortable because they fear disappointing others or being seen as uncooperative. However, saying "yes" to every request often leads to overwhelm, stress, and burnout. When you say "no" to things that don't align with your priorities, you're actually saying "yes" to your well-being, goals, and happiness.

Remember that saying "no" is not a rejection of the person making the request; it's a choice to prioritize what matters most to you. Practice saying "no" by starting with smaller requests, such as turning down an invitation to an event you don't have the time or energy for. You don't need to over-explain or apologize excessively; a simple, polite "I'm unable to commit to that right now" is often enough.

Saying "no" also becomes easier when you have a clear understanding of your values and priorities. When you know what truly matters to you, you can make decisions that align with those values, rather than making choices out of guilt or obligation. This clarity empowers you to set boundaries that honor your needs, helping you feel more balanced and fulfilled.

Communicating Boundaries Effectively

Setting boundaries is essential, but it's equally important to communicate them effectively. Clear, respectful communication helps others understand your limits, creating an environment of mutual respect and understanding. When communicating boundaries, be honest but kind. Use "I" statements to express your needs without placing blame or guilt on others.

For example, if a friend often calls you late at night and disrupts your rest, you might say, "I really value our conversations, but I need to prioritize my sleep. Could we catch up earlier in the evening?" This approach communicates your boundary while still expressing appreciation for the relationship.

When setting boundaries, be prepared for various reactions. Some people may respect your boundaries immediately, while others may resist or feel hurt. Remember that how others respond to your boundaries is not your responsibility; your responsibility is to honor your own needs with kindness and consistency. Setting boundaries may feel challenging at first, but the more you practice, the more confident and empowered you'll become.

Overcoming Guilt and Fear of Disapproval

One of the most common obstacles to setting boundaries is the fear of disappointing others or being perceived as selfish. Many of us are taught to prioritize others' needs over our own, creating a sense of guilt when we choose to focus on ourselves. However, prioritizing your well-being is not selfish, it's an essential part of living a balanced and healthy life.

To overcome guilt and fear of disapproval, remind yourself that setting boundaries allows you to show up more fully in your relationships. When you're constantly overextending yourself, you risk burnout, which can negatively impact your ability to be present for others. By honoring your own needs, you can contribute to your relationships from a place of wholeness and authenticity.

It's also helpful to recognize that not everyone will understand or agree with your boundaries, and that's okay. Boundaries are personal, and they're meant to protect your well-being, not please others. Trust that those who truly care about you will respect your limits, even if they don't fully understand them. The right people will appreciate your honesty and respect the fact that you value yourself enough to set boundaries.

Creating Space for Self-Care and Personal Growth

Setting boundaries is more than just saying "no." It's creating space for the things that nourish and fulfill you. When you set boundaries, you free up time and energy that can be dedicated to self-care, personal growth, and the pursuits that bring you joy. This might mean carving out time each week for a hobby you love, setting aside moments for reflection, or prioritizing activities that support your physical and emotional health.

Consider what you want more of in your life. Maybe it's time for creativity, time to learn something new, or simply time to rest. Boundaries allow you to create a life that feels intentional and meaningful, aligning your daily routines with what genuinely matters to you. By protecting this space for self-care and growth, you nurture a sense of fulfillment that extends into all areas of your life.

Embracing Flexibility and Reassessing Boundaries

Boundaries are not fixed; they're dynamic and may evolve as your life changes. It's important to periodically reassess your boundaries to ensure they continue to serve you. Life is full of shifts, new responsibilities, relationships, and goals that may require you to adjust your boundaries to maintain balance.

For instance, a boundary that worked for you in a demanding job might need to be redefined if you switch careers or enter a new relationship. Embracing flexibility allows you to adapt your boundaries to your current needs, keeping your life balanced and aligned with your well-being.

Reassessing boundaries also helps you notice where you might have become too rigid. Sometimes, in an effort to protect ourselves, we create boundaries that feel isolating or restrictive. Practicing flexibility means evaluating whether your boundaries are supportive or limiting, and then adjusting as needed. This process keeps your boundaries intentional and responsive to the ever-changing journey of self-discovery and personal growth.

Reflection Exercise : *Setting Boundaries and Honoring Your Needs*

Take time to reflect on your relationship with boundaries and self-care. Use the following questions as journaling prompts or personal reflections to deepen your understanding of what boundaries you may need to set and how you can honor your needs.

1. What areas of my life feel overwhelming or draining, and what boundaries could help alleviate that?

2. Are there any patterns of saying "yes" out of guilt or obligation, and how can I practice saying "no" with confidence?
3. What needs are essential to my well-being, and how can I prioritize them in my daily life?
4. How can I communicate my boundaries clearly and kindly to those around me?
5. How do I feel when I set boundaries, and what reminders can help me overcome guilt or fear?

These reflections will guide you in setting boundaries that protect your energy, prioritize your well-being, and empower you to live a life that feels balanced and fulfilling. Boundaries are not a form of selfishness; they're a form of self-respect, a way of saying, "I value myself and my needs." As you honor these boundaries, you create a life that aligns with your true self, allowing you to thrive and contribute meaningfully to the world.

In the next chapter, we'll explore how to nurture self-love and acceptance as foundational elements of personal growth, helping you embrace your strengths and imperfections on this transformative journey.

"I forgive myself, I accept myself,
and I choose to love myself deeply."

CHAPTER 8

NURTURING SELF-LOVE AND ACCEPTANCE

"Embracing who you are is the first
act of love; nurturing that acceptance
is the journey of a lifetime."
—Quan Thomas

As you journey through self-discovery, resilience, and boundary-setting, you arrive at key aspects of personal growth: self-love and acceptance. These pillars ground you in compassion and allow you to embrace both your strengths and imperfections. Self-love means honoring your worth and showing yourself kindness, even in moments of struggle. Acceptance is the ability to see yourself clearly and embrace all parts of who you are—your talents, your quirks, and even your flaws.

In a world that often emphasizes self-improvement, it's easy to feel like you're never "enough." But self-love and acceptance go beyond achieving perfection; they're about learning to love yourself as you are, recognizing your inherent worth, and allowing that acceptance to become a foundation for growth. This chapter is an invitation to release the need for approval, replace self-criticism with compassion, and build a relationship with yourself rooted in understanding, empathy, and grace.

Why Self-Love and Acceptance Matter

Self-love and acceptance are essential for emotional resilience, inner peace, and overall well-being. You become less dependent on external validation when you love and accept yourself. Regardless of others' opinions, you trust your worth and approach life's challenges with a sense of calm and self-assuredness. Self-love gives you the confidence to try new things, take risks, and pursue your dreams, knowing that your worth doesn't depend on the outcome.

Self-acceptance also allows you to see yourself honestly. Rather than hiding or downplaying your flaws, you embrace them as natural parts of being human. This doesn't mean giving up on growth; instead, it means that you approach growth from a place of compassion, not criticism. When you accept yourself, you create a space for authentic growth, free from the constant pressure to be someone you're not.

This, in turn, leads to a more fulfilling life, as you begin to live in alignment with your true self.

Recognizing and Releasing Self-Criticism

One of the biggest obstacles to self-love and acceptance is self-criticism. Many of us have an inner critic, a voice that points out our perceived flaws, criticizes our choices, and makes us feel inadequate. This voice can be harsh and unkind, often leaving us feeling defeated or insecure. While self-criticism can sometimes motivate us to change, it usually leads to feelings of shame and self-doubt, making it harder to embrace our true selves.

To cultivate self-love, it's important to recognize this inner critic and consciously choose a kinder, more compassionate approach. Start by noticing when self-critical thoughts arise. Often, these thoughts are automatic, so it can take practice to become aware of them. When you catch yourself being critical, pause and ask, "Would I speak to a loved one this way?" If the answer is no, reframe the thought in a more compassionate way.

For example, instead of thinking, "I failed again; I'm so useless," try saying, "I made a mistake, but I'm learning and growing." This shift in language may feel small, but it can profoundly impact how you see yourself. Over time, replacing self-criticism with self-compassion becomes second nature, helping you build a more loving and supportive relationship with yourself.

There was a moment when I realized the person I needed to apologize to was me. For every time I ignored my own needs. For silencing my voice. For being my harshest critic. So I did it. I stood in the mirror, placed my hand on my heart, and whispered, 'I'm sorry. I love you. I forgive you. That small moment shifted something in me. It was the beginning of treating myself not as a project to fix— but a person to love.

Practicing Self-Compassion

Self-compassion is the practice of treating yourself with kindness, especially when you're struggling, facing a setback, or feeling inadequate. It's recognizing that everyone has moments of imperfection, and rather than judging yourself harshly, you offer yourself understanding and empathy. Self-compassion is essential for self-love and acceptance because it allows you to see your challenges as part of the human experience, rather than a personal failure.

To cultivate self-compassion, start by acknowledging your feelings without judgment. If you're feeling disappointed, anxious, or frustrated, give yourself permission to feel these emotions without trying to push them away or criticize yourself for having them. Then, remind yourself that these feelings are normal—that everyone experiences similar struggles at times.

A helpful practice for building self-compassion is to place your hand on your heart, take a deep breath, and say, "It's okay. I'm doing my best, and I deserve kindness." This simple gesture can help you reconnect with your inner self, providing comfort and support in difficult moments. Self-compassion is not about excusing mistakes or avoiding responsibility; it's about acknowledging that you deserve kindness, especially from yourself.

Practical Affirmations and Self-Compassion Exercises

Affirmations and self-compassion exercises are powerful tools for cultivating self-love and acceptance. When practiced consistently, they help reshape our inner dialogue and encourage a kinder, more supportive relationship with ourselves.

Examples of Affirmations:

1. For Self-Worth:

   "I am worthy of love and respect just as I am."

   "I bring unique strengths to the world, and I embrace them."

"My worth is not defined by my achievements or others' opinions."

Use these affirmations each morning or during moments of self-doubt. Repeating them regularly helps reinforce a strong sense of self-worth, regardless of external validation.

2. For Self-Compassion:

"It's okay to make mistakes; I am learning and growing."

"I am gentle with myself and honor my journey, no matter where I am."

"I forgive myself for past choices and embrace the person I am becoming."

These affirmations remind you to approach yourself with kindness, especially during challenging times. Use them when feeling self-critical or overwhelmed.

3. For Inner Strength and Resilience:

"I have the strength to overcome any challenge."

"I am resilient, and I learn from every experience."

"Each step I take brings me closer to my true self."

These affirmations are helpful during times of adversity, encouraging you to focus on your inner strength and capacity for growth.

Self-Compassion Exercises:

1. Self-Compassion Break:

   When feeling stressed or self-critical, place your hand on your heart, take a deep breath, and say, "I am doing my best, and that's enough." This simple action offers comfort and helps you connect with a sense of kindness toward yourself.

2. Daily Self-Appreciation Practice:

   At the end of each day, write down three things you appreciate about yourself, such as acts of kindness, small achievements, or moments of resilience. This exercise fosters gratitude for yourself and reinforces positive self-regard.

3. The "Kind Friend" Exercise:

When you notice self-critical thoughts, ask yourself how you would speak to a friend in the same situation. Redirect that supportive language toward yourself, offering understanding and encouragement rather than judgment.

4. Compassionate Breathing:

Take a few deep breaths, focusing on inhaling self-compassion and exhaling self-doubt or judgment. Visualize each breath bringing in kindness and calm, helping you release tension and create a sense of inner peace.

These exercises and affirmations can be incorporated into your daily routine, gradually strengthening your relationship with yourself. Over time, they create a supportive foundation for self-love, helping you build resilience, inner peace, and a more compassionate outlook.

Embracing Your Imperfections

Self-acceptance involves embracing your imperfections with a sense of understanding and grace. In a world that often celebrates perfection, it can be challenging to see flaws as anything other than weaknesses. But imperfection is what makes us human. It's a reminder that we're all learning, evolving, and growing. By accepting your imperfections, you create space to see them as opportunities for growth and self-discovery instead of obstacles.

Think of imperfections as the unique aspects of your character that add depth and richness to your life. Perhaps you're sensitive, easily distracted, or struggle with setting boundaries. These traits, while challenging, are also the qualities that shape your unique journey. Sensitivity, for example, may lead you to be more empathetic and compassionate, while a struggle with boundaries might prompt you to cultivate self-respect and assertiveness.

To embrace your imperfections, practice reframing them in a positive light. Instead of focusing on what you lack, consider how your traits contribute to your strengths. What might these imperfections teach you about yourself or life? Embracing your imperfections doesn't mean you stop working on yourself; it means you approach growth from a place of acceptance, knowing that your worth is not defined by your flaws.

Building a Practice of Self-Love

Self-love isn't just a feeling; it's an active practice that requires intentionality and commitment. Building a practice of self-love involves nurturing yourself in ways that support your well-being and affirm your worth. Here are some ways to incorporate self-love into your daily life:

Set aside time for self-care: Prioritize activities that nourish your mind, body, and soul. This could mean spending time in nature, reading, meditating, or engaging in a creative hobby. Self-care isn't indulgent; it's essential for your overall well-being.

Celebrate small wins: Self-love means acknowledging your efforts and progress, no matter how small. Each day, take a moment to recognize something you accomplished, whether it's completing a task, practicing patience, or learning something new. Celebrating small wins reinforces a positive self-image and reminds you of your growth.

Treat yourself with kindness: Practice speaking to yourself in a way that is supportive and loving. When you make a mistake or fall short, remind yourself that growth is a journey, not a destination. Choose words that affirm your worth and encourage you to keep going.

Surround yourself with positivity: Spend time with people who uplift and support you. Healthy relationships contribute to self-love by creating an environment of respect and encouragement. If you find yourself surrounded by negativity or criticism, it's okay to set boundaries to protect your peace.

Building a practice of self-love may feel challenging at first, especially if you're used to being hard on yourself. But with time and consistency, self-love can become a natural part of your life, providing a foundation of support that strengthens your confidence, resilience, and sense of inner peace.

Accepting Yourself as a Work in Progress

One of the most fulfilling aspects of self-love and acceptance is the realization that you are a work in progress. Growth is not linear, and there will always be areas where you can improve or challenges you need to work through. Accepting yourself as a work in progress means embracing your current self and the person you are becoming, with all the imperfections and potential that come with it.

This mindset helps you see setbacks not as failures but as opportunities for learning and growth. When you approach life with the understanding that you don't have to have it all figured out, you free yourself from the pressure of perfection. Instead, you open yourself up to continuous growth, knowing that each day brings new insights and opportunities to become more aligned with your true self.

Think of self-love and acceptance as a journey rather than a destination. Each day, you can practice kindness, honor your needs, and celebrate the unique person you are. As you accept yourself as a work in progress, you build a foundation of self-love that empowers you to navigate life with confidence, resilience, and authenticity.

Self-Love Truth: "I release the need to be perfect. I am already worthy of love—especially from myself."

From this day forward, I choose to treat myself with the same compassion I've given others. I am not my past. I am not my pain. I am free to love myself fully, gently, and without apology.

Journal Exercise: Nurturing Self-Love and Acceptance

To deepen your practice of self-love and acceptance, take time to reflect on these questions. Use them as journaling prompts or moments of introspection, allowing yourself to explore your relationship with yourself with honesty and compassion.

1. How do I currently speak to myself, and how can I make my inner dialogue more supportive and loving?
2. What are some small acts of self-care that bring me joy and help me feel connected to myself?
3. In what ways can I practice self-compassion, especially in moments of struggle or disappointment?

4. What are some imperfections or quirks I have, and how might they contribute to my strengths or unique perspective?
5. How can I celebrate my growth and progress, even as I continue working toward my goals?

Each reflection is an opportunity to build a deeper, more loving relationship with yourself. As you embrace self-love and acceptance, you create a foundation of compassion and understanding that supports you through life's challenges and joys alike. Remember that self-love is not a destination but a journey, a continuous commitment to honoring your worth, embracing your imperfections, and living authentically.

In the next chapter, we'll explore how to cultivate meaningful connections with others, using the foundation of self-love and acceptance to build meaningful connections.

"I attract relationships that honor,
support, and reflect the real me."

CHAPTER 9

CULTIVATING MEANINGFUL CONNECTIONS

"True connection grows not from the
time spent together, but from the depth
of understanding shared between hearts."
—Quan Thomas

Human connection is one of the most fulfilling aspects
of life. The relationships we form with others bring
us joy, comfort, and growth. Additionally, they
provide the support we need to navigate life's challenges.
Meaningful connections aren't about quantity but quality—
relationships where we feel seen, heard, and valued. As we
cultivate a healthy relationship with ourselves, we can also
deepen our connections with others, building relationships
that align with our values and enrich our lives. This chapter
explores what it means to create meaningful connections,

how to nurture them, and why they're essential for a fulfilling life.

Authentic relationships start with authenticity within ourselves. When we are true to ourselves, we naturally attract people who respect and appreciate us for who we are. Meaningful connections are about more than just shared interests; they're rooted in mutual respect, trust, and genuine care. Building these connections takes time and effort, but the rewards are profound: a sense of belonging, support, and love that fills life with richness and resilience.

The Importance of Connection

Connection is fundamental to well-being. Studies show that people with strong social relationships tend to be happier, healthier, and more resilient. Humans are inherently social beings, and meaningful relationships provide a sense of purpose, fulfillment, and support. When we feel connected, we're better equipped to face life's challenges and celebrate its joys.

Meaningful connections also help us grow. Through our relationships, we learn about ourselves, develop empathy, and gain insight into other perspectives. We're challenged to communicate, compromise, and collaborate, building skills that strengthen our resilience and deepen our self-awareness. Authentic connections create a safe space for vulnerability, allowing us to share our true selves and experience the comfort of being accepted, even with our imperfections.

Building Authentic Relationships

Authenticity is the foundation of meaningful connections. When we show up as our true selves, open, honest, and genuine, we invite others to do the same. Authenticity means being honest about who you are, your feelings, and your values. It's about removing masks and allowing yourself to be vulnerable, which is essential for building trust and creating deep connections.

To build authentic relationships, start by practicing vulnerability. Vulnerability is the willingness to share your true self, even when it feels uncomfortable. When you allow yourself to be vulnerable, you show others that it's safe to be genuine with you. This doesn't mean sharing every detail of your life with everyone you meet, but rather being open with those you trust and letting them see the real you.

Another key to authenticity is consistency. People feel secure in relationships when they know they can rely on you. Show up as you are, be consistent in your actions, and communicate openly. Authenticity is not perfectionism. It means being true to yourself and honoring your values in your relationships. This foundation of honesty and trust creates a space for meaningful connections to grow.

Practicing Active Listening

Listening is a powerful tool in building meaningful connections. Active listening involves being fully present, showing genuine interest, and allowing the other person to express themselves without interruption or judgment. When we truly listen, we demonstrate respect and empathy, creating a safe space for open and honest communication.

To practice active listening, focus on the person speaking. Put away distractions, maintain eye contact, and use body language that shows you're engaged. Avoid interrupting or thinking about your response while they're speaking; instead, give them your full attention. Active listening also involves empathy—try to understand their perspective, even if it's different from your own.

After they've shared, respond thoughtfully. Show that you've understood their message, and ask open-ended questions if you want to know more. Repeating what they've said can also show that you're genuinely interested in their experience. When people feel heard they feel valued, and this fosters deeper, more meaningful connections.

Setting Healthy Boundaries in Relationships

Boundaries are essential in creating healthy, sustainable connections. They protect your well-being and ensure that your relationships are based on respect and mutual understanding. Healthy boundaries allow you to give and receive support without feeling overwhelmed or drained, helping you maintain balance in your life.

To set boundaries, start by identifying what feels comfortable and sustainable for you. Consider your emotional, mental, and physical limits. Do you need personal time to recharge, or do you prefer clear communication around availability? Once you understand your needs, communicate them clearly and kindly.

For example, if a friend frequently calls during your busiest hours, you might say, "I value our conversations, but my afternoons are really busy. Could we plan a time to talk when I can be fully present?" Setting boundaries isn't about pushing people away; it's about creating a structure that supports healthy, balanced relationships. When boundaries are respected, relationships feel more secure, fostering trust and longevity.

Cultivating Empathy and Compassion

Empathy and compassion are the cornerstones of meaningful connections. Empathy is the ability to understand and share someone else's feelings, while compassion involves a desire to support them in their struggles. Both empathy and compassion deepen relationships by fostering understanding, kindness, and a sense of shared humanity.

Cultivating empathy involves putting yourself in the other person's shoes. Instead of judging or offering advice, try to understand what they're experiencing and feeling. This doesn't mean you have to agree with everything they say, but it's about showing that you care and are there to support them.

Compassion goes a step further, inspiring you to offer help when needed. This might mean listening without judgment, offering a kind word, or simply being present. Practicing empathy and compassion strengthens connections and encourages an environment of acceptance and support, where both people feel safe to express themselves openly.

Nurturing Connections through Small Acts of Kindness

Meaningful connections don't always require grand gestures. Often, they're built through small acts of kindness and thoughtfulness. These gestures show that you care, think about the other person, and value their presence in your life. Small acts of kindness can range from sending a quick message to check in, remembering important dates, or simply expressing gratitude for their friendship.

Consistency is key in nurturing relationships. Small, consistent acts of kindness create a foundation of trust and appreciation. Taking time to connect, even briefly, helps maintain closeness and keeps the relationship strong. In today's busy world, a thoughtful message, a warm smile, or a few moments of undivided attention can go a long way in deepening your connection with others.

When we make an effort to show kindness regularly, we strengthen our relationships and contribute positively to the lives of those we care about. These acts of kindness often inspire others to pass on the kindness, creating a cycle of support and connection.

Allowing Space for Growth and Change

Healthy relationships allow room for growth and change. As individuals grow, their needs, interests, and perspectives may evolve. Meaningful connections adapt to these changes with openness and respect. Allowing space for growth means supporting each other's personal journeys, even if they lead in different directions.

To nurture relationships that allow for growth, practice open communication and acceptance. Encourage each other to pursue passions, try new things, and explore different perspectives. Change is a natural part of life, and relationships that can adapt to it tend to be stronger and more resilient.

In some cases, growth may mean moving apart or changing the nature of the relationship. This can be difficult, but it's important to honor each person's journey. If a relationship evolves or ends, trust that the connection served a purpose and added meaning to both of your lives.

By allowing space for growth, you create relationships that are flexible, supportive, and rooted in mutual respect.

Some of the hardest goodbyes aren't angry—they're quiet. As you grow, you may outgrow spaces, conversations, and even people. That doesn't make you disloyal or difficult—it means you're healing. Connection that honors who you are becoming will always feel like alignment, not obligation. It's okay to release what no longer fits.

Connection Truth: "I attract connections that honor who I am—not who I pretend to be."

I release relationships that require me to shrink, silence myself, or settle. I give myself permission to be seen, valued, and loved in the fullness of my truth.

Journal Exercise: Cultivating Meaningful Connections

Take a few moments to reflect on your relationships and how you can deepen your connections with others. Use these questions as journaling prompts or points for personal reflection.

1. What qualities do I value most in my relationships, and how can I foster these qualities in my connections with others?

2. How can I practice authenticity in my relationships, allowing others to see my true self?

3. Are there ways I can improve my listening skills to make others feel more valued and understood?

4. What boundaries do I need to set in my relationships to protect my well-being and maintain balance?

5. How can I incorporate small acts of kindness into my relationships, showing others that I care and appreciate them?

These reflections will help you cultivate meaningful connections based on trust, respect, and genuine care. Meaningful relationships are not just about spending time together; they're about creating a safe space for vulnerability, growth, and mutual support. As you invest in these connections, you'll find that your relationships become a source of strength, joy, and inspiration, enriching your journey and making life's experiences more meaningful.

In the next chapter, we'll explore how to cultivate a life of purpose and fulfillment, aligning your actions and goals with the values and passions that bring you true happiness.

"I live with intention. My purpose unfolds with every step I take."

CHAPTER 10

CREATING A LIFE OF PURPOSE AND FULFILLMENT

"A fulfilling life is not built on what we accumulate, but on the purpose and passion we pour into each day."
—Quan Thomas

Throughout the journey of Rediscovering You, you come to an essential question: What truly brings fulfillment and purpose to my life? Purpose is a guiding force, a sense of direction that gives meaning to your days and aligns your actions with your values. Fulfillment, on the other hand, is the deep satisfaction that comes from living in alignment with this purpose, knowing that your life reflects who you truly are. In this final chapter, we'll explore how to identify and cultivate a sense of purpose, and how to bring a sense of fulfillment into your everyday life.

Creating a life of purpose and fulfillment is a lifelong journey, one that requires continuous self-reflection, growth, and adaptability. Purpose doesn't always have to be grand or tied to a career; sometimes, it's found in simple joys, connections, or moments of service to others. Fulfillment arises when you're able to embrace your unique journey, celebrate your growth, and find meaning in the big and small moments alike. This chapter is an invitation to design a life that brings you genuine joy, fulfillment, and a lasting sense of purpose.

Discovering Your Purpose

Finding purpose begins with self-awareness. Purpose is deeply personal, rooted in your values, passions, and experiences. It's not always a single mission or goal; it's the guiding principle that gives you direction and makes life feel meaningful. Purpose can change over time as you grow and evolve, adapting to new interests, relationships, and experiences.

To discover your purpose, start by exploring what you're naturally drawn to—activities, causes, or interests that feel meaningful to you. Reflect on the moments when you've felt most alive or fulfilled. Were you helping others, creating something, learning, or solving a problem? These experiences often reveal clues about what drives you at a deeper level. ***Ask yourself:***

What activities or topics make me lose track of time?

What issues or causes do I feel passionate about?

What unique gifts, skills, or talents do I bring to the world?

How do I want to impact others or contribute to the world?

Purpose doesn't have to be tied to one singular goal. You may find that your purpose is a blend of multiple passions, such as caring for others, creating art, or advocating for change. Embrace this multi-dimensional purpose, knowing that your unique combination of talents and interests makes your path meaningful.

Aligning Your Actions with Your Purpose

Once you have a clearer sense of your purpose, the next step is aligning your actions with it. Living in alignment with your purpose means making intentional choices that reflect your values and goals. This alignment brings a sense of peace, as your daily life begins to resonate with what truly matters to you. Even small actions, when aligned with your purpose, can bring a sense of fulfillment and joy.

To align your actions with your purpose, consider setting goals that reflect your passions and values. These goals don't have to be big or ambitious; sometimes, it's the small, consistent actions that bring the greatest sense of purpose. For example, if your purpose involves helping others, you might set a goal to volunteer regularly, support a cause, or lend a hand to those in your community. If your purpose is rooted in creativity, you might dedicate time each week to writing, painting, or working on a project that inspires you.

Remember, alignment is not about perfection. Life is dynamic, and there will be times when you feel off-course. In these moments, take a step back, reflect, and make adjustments as needed. Realigning with your purpose is an ongoing process, one that evolves as you grow and change. Each small step you take toward purpose-driven living reinforces your sense of fulfillment and gives your life a deeper sense of meaning.

Cultivating Fulfillment in Everyday Moments

While purpose can guide your life, fulfillment is something you can cultivate daily. Fulfillment comes from appreciating the present moment, finding joy in small acts, and creating a life that brings you contentment and satisfaction. It's about being grateful for what you have while working toward your goals, recognizing that fulfillment is a journey rather than a destination.

One of the simplest ways to cultivate fulfillment is to practice gratitude. Gratitude shifts your focus from what you lack to what you have, helping you recognize the abundance in your life. Take a few moments each day to reflect on things you're grateful for—your relationships, your health, your accomplishments, or even the small joys that brought you happiness that day. By practicing gratitude regularly, you train your mind to focus on the positives, enhancing your sense of fulfillment.

Another way to cultivate fulfillment is to engage fully in whatever you're doing, no matter how mundane. Practice mindfulness by bringing your full attention to the present moment, whether you're working, spending time with loved ones, or relaxing. Fulfillment arises when you savor these moments, appreciating the richness of your experiences without always seeking something more.

Embracing a Growth Mindset

Living a life of purpose and fulfillment requires a growth mindset—the belief that you are always learning, evolving, and capable of growth. A growth mindset allows you to see challenges not as obstacles but as opportunities to learn and improve. This mindset encourages resilience, curiosity, and a sense of openness to life's many possibilities.

With a growth mindset, setbacks and failures are no longer viewed as dead ends but as stepping stones on your journey. When things don't go as planned, ask, "What can I learn from this experience?" or "How can this challenge help me grow?" By reframing difficulties as opportunities for growth, you build resilience and strengthen your sense of purpose.

Adopting a growth mindset also means celebrating progress rather than perfection. Each small step toward your goals, each lesson learned, and each moment of self-awareness is worth acknowledging. Growth doesn't happen overnight, and fulfillment is not a single destination. Embrace the process, knowing that every step forward, no matter how small, brings you closer to a life of purpose and fulfillment.

Serving Others as a Path to Fulfillment

One of the most powerful ways to find purpose and fulfillment is through service to others. When you contribute to the well-being of others, you experience a sense of connection, empathy, and purpose that enriches your life. Service doesn't have to be grand or public; it can be as simple as helping a friend, volunteering in your community, or offering a listening ear to someone in need.

Service allows you to look beyond yourself, bringing perspective and gratitude into your life. It reminds you that you are a part of something larger, and your actions have a positive impact. Acts of service foster meaningful connections, deepen your empathy, and provide a sense of purpose that's rooted in kindness and compassion.

To incorporate service into your life, start by considering ways you can support those around you. It could be volunteering your skills, donating time or resources, or simply offering kindness to others. When you make service a regular part of your life, you create a cycle of giving and receiving that nourishes both you and those you help, enhancing your sense of purpose and fulfillment.

Creating a Vision for Your Life

In my book *Manifest Your Destiny*, I talk about the importance of why you need to Write it, See it, Believe it. In my opinion, these are the first steps to creating a vision for your life. Living with purpose and fulfillment becomes easier when you have a clear vision of the life you want to create. A vision is an inspiring picture of your ideal future, one that reflects your values, passions, and goals. It's not about rigid planning but setting an intention for the life you want to lead. Your vision acts as a compass, guiding your choices and actions, helping you stay aligned with your purpose.

To create a vision for your life, start by asking yourself what you want to experience, contribute, and achieve. Think about the kind of relationships you want, the impact you want to have, and the ways you want to grow. Imagine your ideal day, filled with activities, people, and goals that bring you joy and fulfillment. Let yourself dream without limitations, creating a vision that feels inspiring and true to who you are.

Write down your vision, and keep it somewhere you can see regularly. This vision will remind you of what's most important to you, motivating you to make choices that bring you closer to that life. Remember, a vision is not about creating a strict plan; it's about setting a direction, remaining open to growth, and adapting as you continue to learn more about yourself and what brings you fulfillment.

I used to think purpose had to be big—some grand title, role, or stage. But I've found that the most purposeful moments are the small ones: The way I show up for others. The way I listen. The way I choose peace over performance. Purpose isn't just something you chase—it's something you create daily, by choosing what matters most to you.

Purpose Truth: "I am walking in purpose, even when the path feels unclear."

My life is meaningful. My dreams are valid. Every small, intentional step I take honors the vision placed within me. I don't have to chase purpose—I embody it.

Journal Exercise: Creating a Life of Purpose and Fulfillment

To deepen your understanding of purpose and fulfillment, take a moment to reflect on the following questions. Use them as journaling prompts or moments of introspection, allowing yourself to explore your goals, values, and vision for the future.

1. What brings me a sense of purpose, and how can I incorporate more of it into my daily life?
2. What small actions can I take to align my life more closely with my values and passions?
3. How can I practice gratitude and mindfulness to cultivate fulfillment in my everyday moments?
4. In what ways can I adopt a growth mindset, seeing challenges as opportunities for learning and resilience?
5. What is my vision for a fulfilling life, and what steps can I take to bring this vision to life?

These reflections will help you create a life that feels purposeful, authentic, and fulfilling. Remember, purpose and fulfillment are not destinations to be reached but journeys to be embraced. Each day offers an opportunity to live intentionally, align with your values, and pursue what brings you joy.

As you reach the end of this book, remember that the journey of rediscovery is not a destination but an ongoing process of growth, reflection, and transformation. Each step you take toward understanding yourself, embracing your worth, and aligning with your true purpose is a victory worth celebrating. Life will continue to present challenges, but now you are equipped with the tools to face them with resilience, self-compassion, and clarity. You hold the power to rewrite your story, to honor your unique journey, and to create a life that reflects your deepest values and dreams. Rediscovering you is not about becoming someone new— it's about reconnecting with who you've always been. Trust yourself, stay curious, and continue moving forward with courage and grace. Your best, most authentic self is waiting to unfold.

Rediscovering You Manifesto

I am not here to prove—I am here to *be*.
I give myself permission to rest, heal, grow, and rise.
I honor my boundaries as sacred.
I speak to myself with love and truth.
I walk in purpose, even when the path is unclear.
I am enough—not someday, but now.
I am rediscovering me—and that is more than enough.

For more information visit www.quanthomas.com